D0555720

ISBN 978-1-957600-03-1 (paperback)
ISBN 978-1-957600-04-8 (ebook)

Design- Ivan Petrushevski Flim - flim.mk (cover, typesetting, book),
Katherine MacDonnell (creative direction),
Elena Bojadjieva (book layout),
Maja Tanushoska (creative concept & promotional strategy)
Editorial - Christopher R (content), Marija D (copy), Julia W (proof)

First Edition 2020.
Second Edition 2021.

BAI press
businesssagility.institute

cultivatingtransformations.com

" Transformational Leadership: Connecting the Soulful and the Practical is rich in insight, humor, and hope. From techie to soul guide, London shares lessons from her own journey of discovery, laying out essential elements of soulful transformation in a grounded and pragmatic path. Straight forward yet provocative, this book is packed with wisdom. It is an invitation to act and reflect - so we can transform ourselves and our world. After all, leadership without transformation isn't really leadership, is it? "

-Sally Parker, TimeZero Enterprises

" Wow, what a book! So much solid and field-tested knowledge to move your life and organization forward. Here's the blueprint for the future of product development consulting that you can use today, with the added bonus of straightforward answers to compelling questions like how to get into the room where it happens or what "next level" leader coaching looks like. And a caution: this book will very likely change you, the way you work and the places where you bring your work... forever. "

- David O. Levine, Principal, Coachingagile.com

" Jardena's book is a personal story of expanding her own vulnerability into strength and nurturing deep reflections into insights on transformational leadership. It is authentic in its rawness, and practical in its intimate invitation for cultivating the new way of approaching self-discovery and human systems. Every chapter reminds me of many creative conversations we had where all the different pieces come together in an inspiring stained glass window of ideas. "

- Nadezhda Belousova, Founder of Evolneo GmbH

cultivatingtransformation.com

" Jardena has combined a deep understanding of agility, the lessons learned from every organization she's ever been a part of, and her strong, inherent business sense to create a powerful guidebook for pursuing the sometimes nebulous concept of transformational leadership. Jardena's soul-baring vulnerability and authentic point of view give us an inside-out look at what an agile leader does, and how she shows up in the world. Straightforward and simple, yet deep and inspiring, I recommend this book for anyone interested in growing into their own Transformational Leadership. "

- Laurie Reuben, PCC, Executive Leadership Coach,
Cheshire Consulting Group, LLC.

" This is the book that you buy and carry around with you everywhere. It's the guide that you should read before you read anything else about leadership. Jardena has taken the core competencies required of every leader looking to lead change in their organization and woven them together in a beautiful tapestry with vivid, real and poignant stories that are easily accessible, memorable and actionable. "

- Marsha Acker, CEO, TeamCatapult and author,
The Art & Science of Facilitation: How to Lead
Effective Collaboration with Agile Teams

" This book is gold, whether you are in leadership or not. For most of us, we spend a lot of time with conflict - be it work or personal life, be whatever the reality of the situation is.
These conflicts cause suffering, and with that comes resistance and denial. Jardena's narrative style of story telling with her practical tools, their applications of experimenting, and the valuable

aptness in working through real world scenarios brings everything together. Whether it is your organization or your relationship - this book builds a brilliant corelation in addressing both, and asks us for a serious and bold commitment. Her learnings bring a different lens of awareness that ignites responsibility and acceptance, and how we should be addressing risks for a transformative state through cultivation of awareness and positive influence. And we all know there's nothing which is worthwhile that comes without any risk. "

- Manoj Khanna, Co-Founder & Managing Partner at Qlevio and Publisher at sntioPress

" Jardena London has written a wonderful book here. For me, it's a must read for leaders who want to marry the wellbeing of the business (its bottom line) with its people's wellbeing. Read this book and learn from someone that cares deeply about leaders making a life-affirming impact on organizations. There is much wisdom here in black and white. "

- TC Gill Co-Active® Business Agility Transformation Lead

" Cultivating Transformations provides a good discussion of aspects of emotional intelligence relevant to leading modern projects. It mixes in a few ideas from lean and provides a valuable set of recommendations. It is told with genuine passion and conviction. I like the stories, and it is a good read many people will find helpful. "

- Mike Griffiths, Co-Founder PMI-Agile Community of Practice, President at LeadingAnswers

cultivatingtransformations.com

With deep gratitude to my clients and coworkers, past and present. You have challenged me in uncountable ways that shaped the ideas in this book.

Table of Contents

cultivatingtransformations.com

WHY DID I WRITE THIS BOOK?

Transformational Leadership is a soulful practice, a practical job, and everything in between. You are breathing new life into an organization, and that life energy comes from the spirit of the people. Transformations are usually designed to improve business results, but what's the point if it doesn't make our lives better?

The author Toni Morrison once said, "If there's a book that you want to read, but it hasn't been written yet, then you must write it." This is the book I needed as a companion, to support me and keep me grounded as I pressed on through the day-to-day of Transformational Leadership.

I'm writing this book for myself, but also for you, because you have a tough job. I've been in your tough job, and I am extending a hand that I hope can help pull you up. At the very least, you will feel less alone and find community with other Transformational Leaders.

Transformational Leadership brings to mind JFK's moonshot quote, "We do not do these things because they are easy, we do them because they are hard!" The nature of transformation is that it's uncharted territory, which means there aren't known answers to most of what you do. I can offer you some tools to get oriented, identify patterns, and work through the challenges without feeling lost and overwhelmed. And ideally, without getting fired.

Why is this such a challenging role?
Leaders new to Transformation often tell me, "I'm not afraid of hard work!" I warn them that this is a different kind of hard work than what they might be used to. It's not hard in a way that extra hours will solve; it's hard in the sense that it will challenge the very essence of who you are. Your self-worth, your ego, your values, these will all come under fire every day. You will be asked to challenge the status quo, and then you'll get smacked for challenging the status quo. You will never know where the landmines are buried. If you are not fully grounded with a strong support network, your chances of survival are low.

This book will give you some tools to be a Transformational Leader, but more importantly, it will help you stay grounded and supported in your work. When it starts to feel like it's you against the world, come back to this book, this community, and find some solace and support.

You don't have time to read all the books out there about leadership, transformations, agile, etc. And it's hard to know which books are right for you. I want to give you the straight truth, the stuff no one else will tell you. My hope is that this book cuts through the B*S* and lays out the good, the bad, and the ugly.

Who is this book for? This book is for anyone who has felt the call to leadership to change their world. 'World' is not defined by size. Changing your world can be in your family, community, workplace, global, or any other scope you are called to. The work of a Transformational Leader is similar across different contexts.

The information and advice in this book are directly from my experience, first-hand successes, and first-hand failures. Combined with things I learned from watching other Transformational Leaders succeed and fail. Is it anecdotal? YES! There are tons of books out there with extensive studies, data, proof, sanitized down to broad, generic, meaningless advice. If you want the scrappy truth, the on-the-ground reality, keep reading.

If you've ever felt like you could help, but no one was listening, or people were resistant to your help, this book is for you. We'll take a close look at the underlying causes of resistance and lack of buy-in, and I'll give you practical tools to overcome it.

You might find yourself emotionally reacting to some of the language I use. I don't mean swear words, well, those too, but I mean words like "Politics" and "Hierarchy" and "Love." If you feel emotionally hooked by these words, GREAT! That's an invitation to explore your reaction. I have sought to avoid corporate-sounding words that dilute their meaning, so some of my language may seem abrupt. Get used to it because a transformation is no place for watered-down language.

I'll offer you a few tips on reading this book, but ultimately, you be you. Jump to whatever you need at the moment. The rest is here for you when you need it. I would recommend that you make space for journaling as you read through the book. I've peppered the book with journaling exercises and ideas I hope you'll find provocative. When something hooks you or gets stuck in your head, go explore it in your journal. And if you want to talk with others, join our Transformational Leader online discussion at CultivatingTransformations.com, or read with a book club!

We will dance together between the soulful and the practical throughout this book.

I invite you to step out onto the dance floor.

MY STORY

Before we get started, I'd like to give you some context on my leadership journey.

Growing up without much money, and during the "greed is good" era of the 80s, I was totally focused on money when I started my career. I chose to study Computer Science and Math because that was where the highest starting salaries were, and I wouldn't have to talk to people. I'm an introvert, and I didn't want a job that required me to be a "people person." My experience with people was that they were unpredictable, but as a programmer, I could control the outcome of my work and get paid well for it. What could go wrong?

At my first job, I found out pretty quickly that IT was the most hated division in the company. We were unable to deliver anything on time, and when we did, it rarely worked as planned. I couldn't understand why these brilliant people who were so smart in college were failing so miserably in the world of work. That was when I first felt called to step into leadership. If I had to put aside my introverted self to solve this "IT problem," then that's what I would do.

After a year in IT, I wanted more action, so I left my first job to become a consultant. Being a consultant is like being thrown into the arena with lions. Not everyone welcomes consultants with open arms, and often I could sense their disdain. I quickly learned to establish credibility. I thought if I knew more than everyone, I would be beyond reproach. That worked with technology for a little while, but I used my knowledge as a shield, which would become my downfall as a leader.

As a consultant, I thought we could fix this "IT problem" by being really good at software. I became a tech project manager and then appointed myself the manager of the other project managers. I was now in a leadership role. My leadership position was based on my growing knowledge and willingness to put myself out there. But people were afraid to approach me because I was always so busy. I was intimidating, and I liked it that way.

Because I was pretty good with technology, I took advantage of the fact that so many companies had IT departments that couldn't get software delivered on time and started my own consulting firm. I found two partners, and at age 27, I was off on an entrepreneurial adventure! We were making money, and that was all that mattered to me.

And here's where I faced my first leadership challenge. I knew how to develop software. But I didn't know how to lead. As a CEO, I had no role models or mentors. Those were the heady days of the dot-com boom, and no one cared much about how you led, there was a pot of gold at the end of the rainbow, and people would withstand anything to get it. If you asked anyone who worked for me for their opinion of me during that time, I'm sure it would be less than flattering. The feedback I got from one employee was that she just didn't ever feel like I cared. This wasn't the last time I would hear this feedback. My response was, "I'm not here to care; you want a friend, get a dog!"

During this time, I was also seeing that the problem with software wasn't software. The problem was in the dynamics between people and between business units. I started to read up on how to have better meetings and tried out some of the techniques on my clients. I read as much as I could on better ways of working and eventually stumbled upon Agile. I hadn't yet connected the dots between the people problem and my contribution to the problem.

I now had three young kids at home, and while my business was thriving, something was missing for me. I was craving personal growth. I felt like I had the potential for something more, something meaningful, and this company wasn't it. I was only 37, but I didn't want this to be my legacy. I couldn't quite put my finger on it, but I knew I needed to leave. Although I had a family to support, I threw caution to the wind and left my own company.

I went into a business that failed, then joined a team that hated me, followed by a job where I got fired. Those years seemed aimless and lost, but through those trials, I would learn important lessons. Eventually, I would emerge as a Transformational Leader. In these pages, I'll share those lessons with you, not so you can avoid them, but so you know when they're happening.

WHAT IS TRANSFORMATIONAL LEADERSHIP?

"Transformational Leadership" means different things to different people, so we'll need to agree on a working definition for the remainder of this book. But before we can define the term, Transformational Leadership, let's start by defining "Transformation."

What is Transformation?

The definition of *Transformation* is "change in form." It is such a buzzword right now because it's becoming apparent that the way companies operate fundamentally needs to change for them to survive. Transformation is not about implementing a new process; this is about foundational change.

Implicit in the Organizational Transformation is the idea of a *Paradigm Shift*. A Paradigm Shift is a change in approach or underlying assumptions. We're not just changing form; we're changing assumptions. Think about the assumptions that have changed in your workplace in the past 20 years. Think about the assumptions people are challenging right now. Here are a few assumptions people are questioning today:

- A good, stable employer will take care of you for life.
- We know what to do. We just need to go do it.
- We need someone to oversee and evaluate people's work.
- Everyone is replaceable and interchangeable.
- We measure success by measuring execution against a plan.
- Work must take place at an office.

We're also seeing a need to Transform from the mechanistic organizations of the industrial era to more adaptive, living organizations. In the past, there was an underlying assumption that organizations were machines that ran on the fuel of people. An organization is more like a living ecosystem made of people. This is a change in form as well as a paradigm change. Creating and leading a living system requires different skills and different structures than leading a machine.

What is Transformational Leadership?

Now that we have established what a Transformation is, what is *Transformational Leadership*? I'm using "Leader" in this context to refer to anyone who takes responsibility for changing their world[1]. Transformational Leadership chooses us; we don't choose it. It's more of a calling than a choice.

A Transformational Leader is part spiritual leader, part work manager, part inspirer, and part community builder.

1 Co-Active Training Institute's definition of leadership. (coactive.com)

Transformational Leaders breathe life into organizations.

Why spiritual leader? I use the word "spiritual" in this context to mean that we are attending to the emotional health and souls of the individuals we lead, as well as the collective soul of the organization. 'Soul' is the essence, the ethos, the spirit, that intangible quality of a person or organization. The difference between a machine and a living system is that a living system has a soul. If we ignore that fact, we cannot have true living systems. The paradigm shift into living systems rests on allowing soul back into the workplace. If we think about a Transformational Leader breathing life into an organization, it becomes clear that it is impossible to do that without attending to the souls of both the individuals and the collective organization.

How do you know if you're a Transformational Leader? You may not have the words "Transformational Leader" in your job title, you may not be 'in charge,' but you are making change, you are pushing against what is popular in order to do what's right. You might be working on an initiative or team officially titled "Transformation," or you might be transforming from within a business unit. You are taking risks for the simple chance to make things better for the company. And it's not that you do it once, it's that you do it every single day. And when you get knocked down, you learn from it, alter your tactic, and you come in the next day and try again.

Why do we need Transformational Leadership?

Many of the same skills that worked for leaders in the past, in mechanistic organizations, actually stifle living, adaptive organizations. The things we rewarded leaders for in the past will no longer serve us in the future. Management activities like directing work, driving deadlines, evaluating people; are now replaced by creating conditions, identity, and clarity.

It's simply impossible to adapt and respond to the rapid pace of change by trying to control all the moving parts. If organizations hope to be adaptive and responsive and operate in a VUCA world (Volatile, Uncertain, Complex, Ambiguous), we must change the paradigm of leadership. The more efficient way is to create conditions where the organization can adapt and respond itself.

The big challenge is that we are re-structuring the airplane while it's in flight. This creates a paradox for a Transformational Leader. You're building a new paradigm while working in the old paradigm. You'll work on getting other leaders to stop evaluating people while being evaluated yourself. Instead of support, somebody will constantly be judging you. As you try to remove artificial deadlines, your boss may ask if you can have that done by Friday. Navigating these waters is tricky. You need to find the stepping stones to the future without getting caught in a riptide. Sometimes it's two steps forward, one step back. As Aaron Dignan says, "find the adjacent possible." There's no honor in drowning while swimming towards a future that's not yet available.

Transformations have a soulful element because people can't thrive without spirit. As someone who has degrees in math, computer science, and business, I would have been voted least likely to write a book that contains soulfulness. But the fact is, it keeps chasing me because it's there whether we like it or not.

Our role as Transformational Leaders is to walk the continuum between the soulful and practical. We use practices to allow the soul to flourish, and we use the soul to create better practices.

We need practical solutions with soulful outcomes. And soulful solutions with practical outcomes.

The Lenses of Transformational Leadership

This book is organized to look at Transformational Leadership through three lenses:

- The "Me",
- The "We"
- The "System"

The "Me" refers to the process of mastering ourselves and all the things we do to get in the way of being an effective leader. We start with the "Me" because otherwise, we risk having the "Me" get in the way while we work on the "We" and the "System." In the first section, we'll address the "Me" "The Me: Master your Domain."

The "We" is about how we interact with others and enable people to interact with each other. We'll start with creating a psychologically safe container for people to thrive in their work. Then we move into how to communicate to inspire and spark action as a leader. And finally, we'll address communication and interpersonal skills that build support outside your team. We address the "WE" in the second section, "The We: Leading Human Systems."

The "System" lens allows us to zoom out and look at the overall organizational system and find where it's hampering the organization's success. The system is what we think of when we think of the work of a Transformational Leader. Some of the things we addressed at the "We" will also attend to at the "System" level, such as emotional intelligence, conflict resolution, and coaching. We'll look at how the organization's use of language could be creating undesired outcomes. And finally, we'll explore some fundamentally different ways of thinking about organizations in ways that will spark change. We address the "SYSTEM" in the final section, "The System: Organizing for Adaptability."

First, let's look inward. We need to get our house in order before we can start leading others.

THE ME:
MASTER YOUR DOMAIN

Before you can lead others, you need to master leading yourself. The idea of leading yourself is nothing new; leadership books and leadership training have been preaching this for years. Then why is it so rare to see a fully grounded, authentic, and emotionally intelligent leader?

Self-Mastery is the key to authenticity. Authenticity means that people can see you and your inner light for who you truly are. Developing authenticity is not about adding anything new to who you are. It's about shedding all the things that are blocking your light from shining.

Intuitively, we know when someone is leading from a place of fear. These are the leaders that you find yourself walking on eggshells around. They will always need to be right, and it's tough to change their view. They blame others when things go wrong. They may be known for intimidating people and pitting people against each other. Have you ever worked with a leader like this? We're going to take a long, hard look in the mirror because we all have moments where we exhibit armored leadership.

As I developed my leadership capability, I tried to incorporate what I thought was good leadership. I thought that strong leaders should be intimidating, unwavering, and authoritative. I proceeded to armor up with knowledge and grew porcupine spines so no one could question me. Because I had an answer for everything, people looked to me for all the answers. I couldn't get my company to grow beyond things I could touch and control. It was exhausting.

It was 2009 when I decided to leave my company. Lehman Brothers had collapsed, the Dow Jones Index had just dropped over 50%, and unemployment was at a 25-year high. Not a great time to reinvent yourself, I bounced around between startups and a large company, looking for a role model and someone to "discover me" and "develop me." I gravitated to larger-than-life people, most of whom had an ego to match. I thought that if I could pick the right person to attach myself to, like a sidekick, I could ride with them into greatness. I tried to make myself "big" like they were, but it never felt right, and I never felt good enough. I was disappointed over and over, I felt misunderstood, and I wasn't able to truly add my own value.

The "great thing" I was searching for didn't seem to have a role model. It wasn't part of someone else's plan. I needed to chart my own course. I was disillusioned with the concept of leadership and decided to focus on the work and stop wasting time managing people. The business world judges leaders by the number of people they manage. I didn't care. I needed a break from management. I didn't know it at the time, but this would allow me the space to start the journey into self-mastery.

I had a colleague whose presence I found magical. I asked her how I could become magical too. She laughed and shared her journey with me. That conversation would change the trajectory of my life.

I had been leading from a place of fear and ego, and it hurt the people around me. My team's main goal became making me feel good or trying to get my approval. When people's energy is going into managing fear and ego, it's not going into other, more productive activities. You might see this when a team puts tremendous energy into making their boss happy. More energy, perhaps, than they put into making the company successful. For every individual un-grounded leader, the company loses energy, and the leader's initiative and goals lose energy. Every second someone spends thinking about what the leader might think is a second of wasted energy that could be going into the work.

What is it like to be around a grounded leader? These are the leaders that make you feel like anything is possible, and your contribution is essential. They bring people together in a way that feels exhilarating. You might notice people seeking opportunities to work with this leader, and they may even follow them if they leave the company. As much as we all have armored moments, we also all have grounded moments. Transformational Leaders always seek to expand their grounded leadership and minimize their armored leadership.

Back to the question, why is it so rare to see grounded leaders? What are the underlying assumptions around how we expect a leader to act? When we see a leader with a big ego, whose team fears them and is in full compliance, we view them as a strong leader. It looks impressive, like clockwork, no one steps out of line, it's neat and clean. The paradigm shift to living systems is that they are messy looking. The leader may not know all the answers. Transformational Leaders help others see the outcomes and not get distracted judging the neatness of the process. Standing in the face of this change is hard. You will face harsh criticism. If you are not grounded in yourself first, you will be eaten alive by sharks.

In that life-changing conversation, my magical colleague told me that her journey started when she attended 'coach training.'. And though I didn't want to be a professional coach, I did it anyway. The first step in becoming a coach is to gain selfawareness. As my journey unfolded, I would quickly learn how little self-awareness I had and the negative impact it had on my effectiveness as a leader.

Self-Awareness

I flew into LA on a windy day in October 2009 to meet with a client. The Santa Ana winds were so fierce as I held tight to my wrap dress for fear it would unwrap before I reached the client's office. My colleague and I both arrived dressed in the New York standard clothing: all black. The first thing the client asks when we walk in is, "who died?" They wore flannel shirts and khakis. At that moment, I could sense that the client didn't want us there. We looked like two hotshot New Yorker consultants, overdressed and overly ambitious. Every time I spoke, he would respond with vitriol. But what I was saying was correct, I was right, and I knew it. Each time he shouted at me, I would say the same thing, maybe with slightly different words, but the same thing. Each time I repeated the information, his face got redder and redder, and he would get angrier and angrier until my fellow consultant finally intervened. As we were leaving the building, my fellow consultant asked me if I noticed the man's adverse reaction to what I was saying. I replied, "Yes, but I was right." He looked me in the eye and gently said, "when you see someone getting angry, you might consider changing your approach." Until that moment, this had never occurred to me that there was more to a conversation than facts. I saw the world in black and white. I lacked any self-awareness of my own impact.

Self-awareness has two dimensions:

- Knowledge of your own emotional reactions.
- Attunement to the impact you have on others.

Self-awareness is a paradox. When someone tells me they are self-aware, I want to yell, "NO! A self-aware person would never say that!" The more self-awareness you gain, the more you realize how much you lack. It's one of those things where each time you learn something, a door opens to a world of things you don't know. It's like a video game; each time you master a level, it unlocks new and more difficult challenges.

"The more self-awareness you gain, the more you realize how much you lack."

Self-awareness is an infinite well of learning because there are big rocks to be aware of, small pebbles to learn, and tiny grains of sand that will fill in your self-awareness for a lifetime. When you think you've advanced to work on sand, another big rock comes along! And as you learn more about yourself, you are continually changing, creating a moving target. For example, when I learned that people saw me as harsh and bossy, I shifted how I showed up. But then I found out that I lost some of my ability to get things done. I had to re-learn how to be effective without being harsh and bossy.

Why is self-awareness important to Transformational Leadership? "If I'm doing a good job, who cares if I'm self-aware or not?" Transformation is not a coin-op machine; it consists of human beings. How you show up matters. Self-awareness allows you to change your impact on other people. If you don't know how you are impacting others or impacting them negatively, transformation won't be possible.

Can you step outside yourself for a moment and see how your presence impacts those around you? Until you can see how you affect the situation, you can't accurately see the situation because your bias clouds it. For years I thought I could attend a meeting as an observer, and it would have no impact on the discussion. I didn't think I mattered; I wasn't speaking, I didn't know anything, who would care? Flip the scenario and think about a time when you were in a meeting, and an observer joined. Did you wonder why they were really there? How did their facial expressions affect the rest of the group? There is no such thing as "no impact," so know your impact.

Here's a little red flag that can help you know when you're ignoring your impact. When I hear myself using language like "I told them.... I shared this ..." and omitting the responses and reactions, I know I've turned off my self-awareness. If my stories are all about "what I said" and don't have a corresponding "what they said" or "how they reacted," I have lost connection to my own impact.

There are many tools out there to help you gain self-awareness. I'll give you a few starters here, but please continue on your own journey.

• Coaching. Getting a coach can help by reflecting things back to you, holding up a metaphorical mirror for you to see yourself better. You can work with them to take action based on what you see. Find a coach that will call you out on your bullshit. If you can get them to see you in the wild (like a staff meeting), even better. Check out CoachFederation.org to find a professional coach.

• Johari Window. This fabulous, free, online tool helps you see your blind spots. It works like this; you enter in some characteristics on how you see yourself, and then you send a link to a bunch of people you know, and they do the same. The tool sorts out how you see yourself that others don't, how you accurately see yourself, and things others see that you don't.
Johari Window - https://kevan.org/johari

• Books. There are many excellent books on this topic. Check out Emotional Intelligence 2.0 and The Anatomy of Peace for a start. Once you get started, you'll find that each book leads you to another.

Self-awareness is key that opened all the other doors for me. Once I started to reflect on my reactions and other people's reactions to me, it was like I'd entered a new world. The way I was showing up impacted the outcome of my work and my team's work. Honestly, it felt pretty crappy when I started to become aware of my bitchy self. I had a choice: I could either retreat into a pit of shame or keep pressing on and try to change it. Always the tenacious one, I pressed on.

Journal Exercise: Take a moment to examine an interaction you had this week. It could be with an individual, or it could be a group. How did the other(s) respond to you? Did the energy shift based on what you said or did? What assumptions did you make to yourself to explain their reactions? What assumptions do you imagine the other people made?

Emotional Literacy

One of the keys to self-awareness is being able to identify and sit with our emotions. Old leadership paradigms told us that there was no place for emotion in leadership. In fact, good leaders were taught not to show emotion unless it was for an intentional purpose, anger for late delivery, sadness over death.

In an effort to be a "strong leader," I learned to suppress my emotions to the point where I could no longer identify them. I was tough, I was strong, I was…well, a bit cold. Then I started working at a company where I was struggling to figure out how to add value. I couldn't quite identify the problem, so I just pressed on, working hard, and trying to be good. One day I was confronted by the all-male executive team, challenging me on what my value was. I broke down in tears. It was not my finest moment. My emotions completely blindsided me; I had no idea that these emotions were lurking just below the surface. Ignoring my emotions allowed the feelings to sneak up and take over. It was almost like the emotions were begging for my attention. One of the things I learned as I recovered from that experience was Emotional Literacy.

Transformational Leaders are not ruled by emotion but rather informed by it. When an emotion shows up, they put language to it instead of having it seep out in dysfunctional behaviors. Emotional literacy doesn't mean that you show all your emotions, it just means that you are aware of them. A traditional leader might hide their fear of late delivery by being hard on the team, blaming, and shaming. A Transformational Leader might simply say, "I fear the impact of late delivery. We stand to lose six big customers, and it could put our jobs at stake. What can we do?" Another Transformational Leader might notice that they fear late delivery, and realizing that there's no evidence for their fear, choose to say nothing. Transformational Leaders develop their ability to discern whether an emotion is intuition or fear.

"Transformational Leaders are not ruled by emotion but rather informed by it."

The first key to emotional literacy is putting language to it. Most humans can only identify 3-6 emotions. According to Bessel Van der Kolk, *The Body Keeps the Score,* "The language and emotion centers of the brains are not near each other. This separation makes putting language to emotion difficult for most people." It will take practice and attention to become attuned to your emotions.

Notice the difference between an emotion and a conclusion. I often find myself saying, "I feel like we're going to be late." That's not actually a feeling; that's a conclusion. The feeling is "fear" or "worry." Feeling attacked, excluded, intimidated are other examples of conclusions, not feelings. When you feel attacked, that's a conclusion you're making about the external world. What's the feeling inside? Maybe you feel anger, sadness, or fear. The distinction between emotion and conclusion sparks a shift away from blame.

Getting more specific about what you're feeling can help you access your emotions and be better able to communicate them to the people around you.

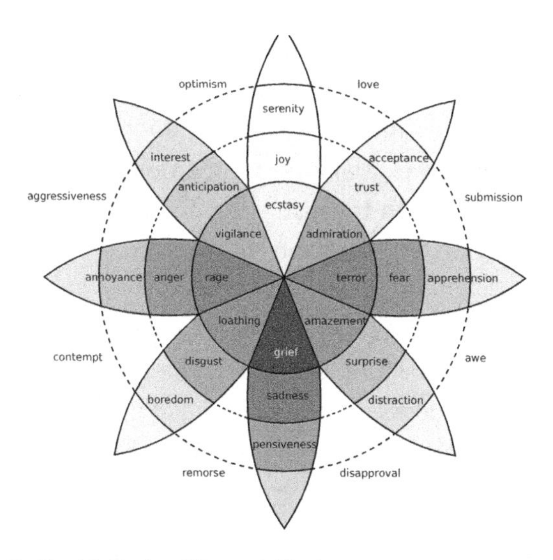

Credit: Plutchik, Machine Elf 1735, Public domain, via Wikimedia Commons.

This handy wheel of emotion helped me learn to articulate my emotions. When you are feeling something, check in with the wheel and see if you can find the word for it. The wheel shows more specific emotions as you move outward on the leaves.

Journal Exercise: Print out a copy of the wheel of emotion[2]. Carry it around with you for a week. Check in with yourself at least three times a day and find your feelings on the wheel. How specific can you get with your emotions? Log them in your journal. What do you notice about naming your emotions?

Now that we've identified our emotions, we need to sit with them and observe them. There is often some confusion between managing our emotions and suppressing them. We want to have emotions; both negative and positive emotions are hugely valuable! But we don't want our emotions to control us and control the people around us. We do want our emotions

2 Machine Elf 1735, Public domain, via Wikimedia Commons. https://commons.wikimedia.org/wiki/File:Plutchik-wheel.svg

to provide information to ourselves and the people around us. Suppressing emotions deprives us of the information the emotion is giving us and can potentially flood us with emotions when the dam bursts. Managing the emotion means that we can allow the emotion to exist, share it, learn from it, but not allow the emotion to be in control.

An emotion only lasts for about 90 seconds, according to neuroanatomist Dr. Jill Bolte Taylor[3]. The rest of the time we spend judging, processing, and reacting to our emotions. If you wait for 90 seconds, the actual emotion will subside. Remind yourself that you are not your emotions. Emotions are fleeting. Once the emotion passes, you can take back control and decide what to do.

Not all emotions come from the brain. Sometimes our body is more attuned to our emotions than our conscious mind. For me, my cheeks get hot several full minutes before my brain knows I'm getting upset. I only recently realized that I could leverage this advanced warning system. In the past, I would feel my cheeks get hot, try to suppress it, and then get surprised by a rush of emotion. Now I take that delay time to get curious about why my cheeks are getting hot. For you, it might be different, you may feel a tightening in your chest, or your hands might get fidgety. Get curious! You're getting an early warning. Listen to it.

As human beings, emotions are designed to give us information. We can get access to a tremendous wealth of information if we listen to our emotions. Be careful not to assign meaning to that information too quickly. Get curious about your own role in the emotion. For example, if I have a strong negative reaction to a job candidate, that's information. It could be that this person

3 Jill Bolte Taylor, TED talk: https://www.ted.com/talks/jill_bolte_taylor_my_stroke_of_insight

is unsuitable, but it might also be that something caused me to feel threatened. I can use the information to tap into what exactly it is that made me feel threatened. Was this person truly unsuitable as a candidate, or was my reaction about my own ego? Emotions are information, but it's not always the information you think it is.

First, you've identified the emotion. That's a big step. Simply practice that for a while. The second step is to get curious about why you have the emotion. And finally, you decide what you want to do about it. Sometimes it helps to share your emotion with others. Sometimes it doesn't. Sometimes an emotion might spark you to take action. And sometimes, an emotion is just an emotion, and there's no action to take.

As for my story, I've gotten much better at seeing my emotions as they arrive. They can still sneak up on me, but I am less surprised. An emotion snuck up on me recently when I was facilitating a workshop about resiliency. I shared this leadership story from 5 years ago: A client had asked me to speak with her leadership team about a Transformation I was leading. After 2 hours of being crammed into a hot, crowded conference room, there were only 4 minutes left, and it was my turn to speak. After 60 seconds, the leader interrupted me and completely undermined the whole initiative by questioning the approach, and then she said, "no need to answer," and ended the meeting! I felt like I got punched in the face! Why did she even hire me? As I was telling this story in my recent workshop, my voice started to crack. This story was from 5 years ago. When I decided to tell it, I hadn't anticipated my emotional reaction. Back when it happened, I didn't even cry or feel any emotion besides frustration. Why was it showing up now? But I have more emotional literacy than I did five years ago, so in the workshop, I was able to name it and say to the group, "Well, I guess I'm still upset about this." I didn't break down in tears, I wasn't embarrassed, I just named it, acknowledged it for the group, and then I continued on.

Journal Exercise: As you sit in your next meeting, see if you can identify an emotion that emerges for you. Get curious. What is this emotion telling you? What, if anything, do you need to do with this information? Jot any insights down in your journal.

Armor & Ego

The messages I heard from a young age were that I needed to shine. Stand out! Be special! Be the best! In a capitalist society, driven by rugged individualism, many of us received these messages. I felt tremendous pressure to live up to my potential. This pressure prompted me to find ways to inflate my ego.

What is Ego? Dictionary.com defines ego as the "I" or self of any person. We think of a "Big Ego" as someone whose sense of self overshadows the needs of others. When does our normal sense of self get in our way?

As a Transformational Leader, it is essential that you realize that everything is not about you. Sounds obvious, right? Why is it so hard to practice?

I told a story earlier about a client that didn't want me there and yelled at me every chance he got. The first time I spoke with him on the phone, I didn't even say a single word, except "Hi, this is Jard…" and he proceeded to scream and swear at me for 15 minutes and then hung up on me. I called my trusty colleague, and I wailed, "But I'm a nice person! He didn't even give me a chance!" Right, he didn't give me a chance. I didn't even speak a word, so how could it possibly be about me? And yet, it felt very personal. It bruised my ego. My colleague asked me, "what do you think might be going on with the client that he would scream at you like that?" I didn't know at the time, but as I would come to discover, quite a lot was going on with him, and none of it had anything to do with me.

I got curious about his reaction. I held back the urge to call this person and tell him what a jerk he was. It was hard because I wanted to assert my power. Everything I was ever taught told me not to appear weak! But I didn't want to fuse my reaction to his reaction. Bar fights start the same way; one person reacts, and someone else reacts to their reaction, and so on.

Work hard to let go of thinking that people's reactions are about you. The truth is that people aren't thinking about you as much as you think they are. We waste a tremendous amount of energy speculating about what other people think of us. Let go of your attachment to their reaction. Get back to making things happen.

Armor is tightly linked to ego, as we create armor to protect our sense of self. When we feel threatened, we protect ourselves by building a layer of emotional armor between ourselves and things that feel bad.

We've been doing this all our lives. It served you well for many years, helped you get through those teen years. In high school, the rebels are a great example of teen armor. Maybe you owned a studded leather jacket and combat boots? Teen rebel clothes even looked like armor! Developing a rebellious attitude protects teenagers from conforming and allows them to explore their own identities. As adults, we build up armor too. The only way I could withstand harsh criticism in some jobs was to armor up. I had to believe that I didn't care what people thought or that they were plain stupid.

"It's not fear that's holding you back; it's armor."
- Brené Brown

When I first heard the term "emotional armor," I asked someone if that was a thing. I had never heard of this. She looked at me for a second and answered, "Oh, it's a thing, and you have a ton of it!" Ouch!

With my armor, I could confidently step into any situation. But what I found out is that confidence isn't connection. Actually, confidence can often block connection. If you've ever heard people say, "They don't like her, but they respect her," this is how it looks when you're confident but not connecting.

At some point, we have built up so much armor that we block people from connecting to us. The same thing that keeps the bad stuff out keeps the good stuff in.

"The trouble with putting armor on is that, while it protects you from the pain, it also protects you from pleasure."
- Celeste Holm

Peeling back your armor may be a lifelong process. As you start to remove layers of armor, you'll likely feel exposed. I remember calling a friend after being undermined by a client in front of a large group and saying, "I want my armor back now!" The thing about armor is that it's always there for you if you really need it. You can summon it like Iron Man. Wearing it all day long is too heavy. And people don't know who you really are. I wanted my armor back that day, but I didn't need it. Instead, I got curious about why this person undermined me.

As for the client screaming at me on the phone earlier, I got curious as to why he was so angry. I found out that he was an entrepreneur whose company was purchased by the larger company where he now worked, and he was frustrated with his new lack of autonomy. He was having trouble fitting in, and now his job was at risk. I was able to work with him in a way that helped heal that anger. We worked together to get some project wins to meet his performance goals, which earned him back some of the freedom he was yearning for. Two months later, he was my biggest advocate!

Journal Exercise: This week, at the end of each workday, take a minute to reflect on your armor. Where did it show up? When did you take it off? What armor did you notice in others?

Deep Curiosity

"I have no special talents. I am only passionately curious."
- Albert Einstein

Curiosity is the antidote to judgment. One of the easiest ways to achieve emotional intelligence is by getting curious. When you aren't sure how you're feeling, get curious. When you aren't sure how someone else is feeling, get curious. Keeping your curiosity open and alive will open up things that weren't possible before.

"Curiosity - asking questions - isn't just a way of understanding the world. It's a way of changing it."
Brian Grazer, A Curious Mind: The Secret to a Bigger Life

Asking Powerful Questions can help you stay curious. Powerful questions are open-ended questions that get the other person thinking and that don't presuppose a solution. We often ask questions because we are trying to lead the other person to our conclusion. Curiosity means that we are looking to grow the space of the conversation rather than shrink it. I like to use the Powerful Questions cards put together by the Agile Coaching Institute[4].

One warning about curiosity, there is a limit. When curiosity becomes interesting but not useful, or not even potentially useful, it's time to stop. While questions can help build a relationship, people like to know you are interested in them. At some point, when you find yourself asking about details that don't matter, it's just wasting time. There's no rule here, just be aware and look for that tipping point. If you're not sure, ask yourself, "why am I asking?" Lean into your self-awareness to sense whether your curiosity is useful.

Journal Exercise: Think of a current relationship you have where there is some difficulty. Next time you see this person, instead of showing them your perspective, see if you can get curious about their perspective. Don't even attempt to represent your view, just this one time. As an aid, you might choose three questions from the Powerful Questions cards ahead of time and use them when you can't think of a question. Notice their reaction. Did it differ from your usual interaction?

Resiliency and Recovery

"The green reed which bends in the wind is stronger than the mighty oak which breaks in a storm."
- Confucius

At this point, we've established the fact that Transformational Leadership is tough work. Tough on the soul, tough on the

4 https://abiggergame.today/wp-content/uploads/PowerfulQuestions_cards_EN1.pdf

ego, tough on the intellect. To withstand this battering, as Transformational Leaders, we need to nourish our souls continually through resiliency and recovery.

Resiliency is the ability to withstand difficult conditions. Think of the reed that bends but doesn't break.

Recovery is the ability to bounce back and refocus after you find yourself hijacked.

Why do we care about all this stuff? If I can suppress my feelings, and get my work done, then what's the difference? The difference is that a) people can see your reactions, even when you think they can't. It leaks out in different ways, but it leaks out. And b) it's going to affect your ability to make good decisions. Hiding, or suppressing, an emotion and recovering from an emotion are two entirely different things.

When you suppress an emotion, it's still there. Recall my earlier story where I broke down crying in an executive meeting. My armor was thick, but once it cracked, there was no resiliency underneath. There's a phrase from Robert Hilliker[5] that sums this up perfectly, "*Hold your shadow in front of you. It can only take you down from behind.*" If you're not facing those emotions, they're just waiting to jump out and surprise you.

There's a myth that you can be so resilient that you'll never have to recover because you never have an emotional reaction. If this ever happens, stick a pencil in your eye to see if you feel it. If you never have an emotional reaction, check in with yourself and see if it's armor that you are mistaking for resiliency. Have you stopped being human? The truth is, you'll always have emotional reactions, and that's a good thing. Emotions give

5 Quote via Brené Brown

us information and intuition that our brains might miss. These feelings connect us to other people. Emotions are the direct line to our soul.

If emotions are so valuable, why do some emotions hijack us and distract us? According to Kristen Neff[6], resistance multiplies our suffering. She uses this simple formula:

SUFFERING = PAIN * RESISTANCE

The more we resist a painful emotion, or any emotion, the more we suffer, and the harder it is to recover. If you've ever had the feeling that you should be happy, but you're not, you'll know what I mean by resistance. Or if you've felt jealous of someone else's success, you know you should be happy for them. So, you squash that feeling and miss the chance to get curious about your jealousy. But your jealousy leaks out in subtle ways because it's still in there. Maybe you criticize the person you're jealous of in an effort to make yourself feel better. Society has a bunch of rules for how we should feel, and when we don't feel that way, we try to make ourselves feel the way we 'should' feel. That's resistance. Acknowledging and then letting go of the judgment and resistance around emotion can exponentially lower our suffering and make it a whole lot easier to recover.

We can supercharge our resiliency and recovery by building two competencies: knowing your self-worth and knowing your values.

Self-worth.

Self-worth is knowing that your presence is valuable and knowing that you are deserving of good things. There's security in knowing that you are worthy. Self-worth doesn't come from

6 Kristen Neff, Self-Compassion.

an accumulation of knowledge. You are not worthless until you get a certification, a degree, or read a particular book. Self-worth is about your being, your soul. You are worthy just by being you. By showing up, your energy is valuable, even if you don't say a word. Other people can feel this groundedness. You can admit mistakes. You can withstand criticism. When you know your self-worth, you are resilient. You don't need to prove anything when you know your self-worth, and you aren't hustling for it. When you know your self-worth, you have a recovery anchor that brings you back to center when you get emotionally hijacked.

> *"If you don't know your self-worth, you will constantly be hustling for it."*
>
> *- Brené Brown*

Consider a situation where an executive is banging their fist on the table, demanding that your approach is wrong, and you must change it. How does this feel if you don't know your self-worth? How quickly will you discard your idea and get in line with the executive's demand? How much wine will it take to help you recover? Now consider how it feels when you know your self-worth. Is it easier to get curious about why this person is having an emotional reaction? Do you recover more quickly? And most importantly, will you end up with a better outcome for the organization? I know that when someone challenges me on an idea when I'm not grounded in my self-worth, I can quickly back down. The problem is that my idea might be worth exploring, but the organization will never have the chance to find out.

Values.

A key element that informs your self-worth is knowing your values. What is important to you? Where are you unwilling to compromise? When you know what's important to you, you start to understand what makes you worthy.

When I speak with people whose job is to promote digital 'clicks' and yet at home, they don't let their kids have any devices. I wonder how they reconcile their values. I'm always astounded by people who spend their free time doing things like volunteering, attending religious services, and coaching kids' sports, only to come into work and do the exact opposite of the values they spent their weekend living. I see people violate their values in decisions to overlook overcharges to customers, sell people things they don't need, promote sugar to children, promote online purchases to children and find ways to get people addicted to digital apps. When I ask about these incongruencies, the response is something like "well, that's how we make money here" or "that's what we're measured on" or my favorite, "this is business, it's not personal."

When you are clear on your values, it keeps you grounded. Seek a job that aligns with your values. I know this is hard because most of us need income to live. Maybe it's not possible today, but if you look, you'll find it eventually. We all know the stories of companies that lost their moral compass. In each case, everyone dropped their values, checked their soul at the door, and complied with the profit goal over everything else.

"The only thing necessary for the triumph of evil is that good men [people] should do nothing."
- Edmund Burke

When you know your values, it sparks your self-awareness when something violates your values. When we are unclear on our values, we are easily swayed and spend a lot of time making decisions. We can spend a tremendous amount of energy trying to justify actions that go against our values. We can redirect this wasted energy in more productive ways. Being clear on your values gives you the grounding to be resilient and quickly recover when something violates them.

"These are my principles, and if you don't like them, I have others."

- Groucho Marx

Tools for Recovery

When it comes to recovering in the moment, a foundation of self-worth and values is essential. There are many 'in the moment tools' to deal with emotional hijacking. I encourage you to find resiliency and recovery tools that work for you. Here are a few that work for me.

Journaling. Writing in a journal is a great way to get the emotions out of your head and body. It keeps them from circling around. It also helps you sort through your reactions visually. It's almost magical how writing it down provides clarity.

Meditation. Meditation is a great tool for both resilience and recovery. Training your brain to observe itself is one of the keys. This helps with resiliency as well as recovery. There are tons of other benefits to meditation, but let's start with just this one.

Box-Breathing. Used by the military, box-breathing, or the 4-part breath, can pull you back to center in 16 seconds. Inhale for 4 counts, hold for 4, exhale for 4, hold for 4. Try it right now. Notice how you feel.

> *5,4,3,2,1*. First aid for panic attacks is to ask the person to use their five senses. But it's not only for panic attacks; this is also a great recovery technique for getting grounded back to self when you feel your emotions pulling on you.
>
> *5 things you can see*
> *4 things you can touch*
> *3 things you can hear*
> *2 things you can smell*
> *1 thing you can taste*

Call a friend, go for a walk, listen to your favorite song, look at a picture of someone you love. Find what works!

Resiliency and recovery are key competencies for Transformational Leaders because you will be in tough situations. Knowing your self-worth and values will give you a foundation to stand on. Working on these competencies is inner work, but the results show in your outer world.

Journal Exercise: What situations challenge your self-worth? What would it take for you to accept that you're worthy without doing a thing?
Narrow down your top 2 values from this values list[7]. What situations cause you to compromise your values? Who can help you uphold them?

Courage

I sat in a meeting with a man who was about to roll out a process to bring ideas from concept to cash. The problem was that the process was missing criteria for approval, and steps

7 https://daretolead.brenebrown.com/wp-content/uploads/2020/02/Values.pdf

to determine priority, allocate capacity, and assign funding. If he rolled it out, it would cause mass confusion and hurt the company deeply. First, I asked if he agreed with my assessment of the negative impact, and he did agree. When I asked him why he would push it anyway, his answer was, "My boss said so, and ya' know, I have a mortgage." You may have seen a similar scene in the movie "The Big Short" as the reason for S&P to rate bad debt instruments as "triple-A," a move that almost brought down the whole US economy. It can happen anywhere.

Now multiply this example of lack of courage by thousands of people. And you have a whole company of people willing to knowingly do the wrong thing. I'm not even talking about morally wrong; I'm talking about wrong for the prosperity and success of the company. Your company is working against itself. And when it does become morally wrong, then the problem extends outside the walls of the company. When people lack courage, we all suffer.

A lot of people consider courage "feeling fear and doing it anyway." Let's dig a little deeper into how courage shows up. Glennon Doyle, the author of Untamed[8], says that "Brave is not asking the crowd what is brave. Brave is deciding for oneself." I'm taking some license to use the words 'brave' and 'courageous' synonymously. Courage is from the Latin root -cor, or heart, literally meaning "from the heart." Courage means that you are listening to your inner voice, your intuition, your inner knowing, standing up and speaking from that voice.

As Transformational Leaders, we stand firm even when it's not popular, or we don't get enough 'likes.' This doesn't mean we're bullheaded or obstinate. It doesn't mean we don't change course in the light of new information. It means that we are always willing to speak the truth, willing to step into the fire.

8 Untamed, Glennon Doyle, 2020.

With the concept-to-cash process I mentioned earlier, they ordered the person with the mortgage to 'lock Jardena in a room until she agrees.' I told him that I refused, in good conscience, to put my name on it as an approver. (A little courage from my side.) He and his boss got approval to override me and moved ahead with the rollout. As predicted, it was a disaster, wasting a massive amount of money and causing the company to fail on their new product strategy. All because one man lacked the courage to stand up to his boss.

Journal Exercise: Think about a few tough decisions you've had to make in the past month. Did you trade what you thought was right for what would make you look good? Did you keep quiet? If you stood firm for what was right, what was the impact? Is there a decision in your near future that will require you to show courage?

Showing Up

Doing the inner work of Transformational Leadership leads right into the connection you have with other people. You can't give what you don't have, so you'll need to be grounded in yourself first and continually introspective.

"How you show up matters."

"How you show up matters." What does it mean to "show up"? Just by walking into a room, you have an impact. Without saying a word, you have an impact. Other people are affected by you, whether you think so or not. Your stance, your facial expression, your voice, it all matters. The intention you have when you enter a meeting, in person or remote. Whether you are distracted or engaged, sends a message. Can you tell the difference between someone attending a meeting begrudgingly, assuming it will be a waste of time, and someone eager to make things happen? What's the impact on the outcome of that meeting if no one wants to be there vs. when everyone wants to be there? You bring that difference every time you show up. And while on the one hand, I'll tell you that it's not all about you. On the other hand, your presence affects the people around you.

Bob Anderson calls this "the leader brings the weather."

> *"You bring the weather as a leader into the team, into the organization, and what is happening around you is a reflection of you."*[9]

At any given moment, you are showing up in a room, in a meeting, whether virtual or in person. It may be just a moment, but it has an impact on the organization and the results.

Journal Exercise: Start to notice how other people show up and how their presence changes the energy of a group. Now, start turning the mirror back on yourself, and notice how you show up and how your energy affects the group. How does the energy change when you enter or when you speak?

Asking for Help

Being able to ask for help is a key leadership skill and a struggle for many of us. Being raised in a culture that values independence and individualism can make it hard to admit when we need help. I am so tenacious that I'll bang my head against the wall forever before I ask for help. What I've discovered is that asking for help has benefits that extend beyond the actual help.

9 Robert Anderson and William Adams, Scaling Leadership, 2019.

People say New Yorkers are rude, but one thing New Yorkers love is giving directions. If you stop someone on the street to ask for directions, three other New Yorkers will stop and try to tell you a better way, and someone will walk you at least partway there. Why is this? It's pride! You've activated their inner hero[10]! They want to show you that they know the ins and outs of their city. And now they're invested in you getting there, so they walk with you.

We think asking for help makes us look weak, but just the opposite is true. Leaders will trust complex projects to someone who will ask for help over someone with more knowledge[11]. They know that no one can know everything, and they are more trusting in someone that will ask for help than someone limited by their current knowledge.

The surprising part of asking for help is that when you ask for help, the other person becomes enrolled in your success. Because they have helped you, they want to make sure you succeed and will do things to make sure you succeed well beyond the help you requested. A friend of mine tried this when he asked his archrival for help. He hated admitting to this person that he needed help, but his rival was his ally from that day forward.

Part of asking for help is teaching people how to be with you. We have the power to help people respond to us in the ways we need. Most of us have had the experience of someone complaining to us, and when we try to help them, they reject every suggestion. The thing is that they didn't want our help; they just wanted to feel heard. When we tried to help, they felt even less heard. I have a friend with a very ill husband. Her

10 Gia Storms

11 Brené Brown

family wants so badly to help, but they have no idea how to be with her. They keep doing things that are irritating her. We talked about teaching them to be with her, and she said that she wished they could just know. I think we all feel that way; we wish people could just know how to give us what we need. Some people intuitively know, but most of us don't. My friend started to teach her family how to be with her. Sometimes they accepted her request, and sometimes they didn't. But when they didn't accept the request, she moved on and asked someone else instead of holding out hope that they would help.

Asking for help works the other way too. When you're not clear what someone wants from you, you can ask, "Do you want me to listen, make suggestions or help you fix it?" You are teaching people how to be with you and how you can help.

Asking for help and teaching people how to be with us are two ways that Transformational Leaders show their inner self to the outside world.

Journal Exercise: Think about something challenging you are facing that you have been trying to resolve alone. Identify one person you can ask for help from and reach out to them. If you don't know enough to know what to ask for, say that. Notice how their engagement shifts the possibilities. Also, notice how asking for help changes your interaction with this person

Positive Regard

"Do you believe that people are doing the best they can, in any given moment?" This question is the litmus test for positive regard. Positive regard means that you believe that, yes, people are doing the best they can in any given moment. Can they do better in the future if they gain a skill, get some rest, and...

and…and? Yes, of course, but positive regard means, right now, with the present conditions, are they doing the best they can? Until you can see people as doing the best they can in any given moment, you cannot extend them positive regard. And until you can extend positive regard to all people, you cannot summon the energy necessary to lead a transformation.

A colleague was complaining about an employee. She said, "He's incompetent, lazy, his work is sloppy! And how is he letting his team run amok?!". When she took a breath, I said to her, "You know, he's doing the best he can, right?" She looked at me kinda funny and walked away frustrated. But she came back to me later that day and said, "I heard what you said. He's doing the best he can. This isn't the job for him. We need to find him work where he can thrive."

"Everybody is a genius. But if you judge a fish by its ability to climb a tree, it will live its whole life believing that it is stupid."

- Albert Einstein

"Don't try to teach a fish to climb a tree. It frustrates you and annoys the fish."

- Corollary to Einstein's Quote

The point here is that fish can't climb trees. Teaching a fish to climb a tree is a losing proposition for both you and the fish. Yes, it's soul-crushing for the fish. But also consider the tremendous amount of energy you are wasting. The fish is doing the best they can, being a fish. The fish is not a climber. "Are you saying we should fire the fish?" If you hired the fish as a tree-climber, then yes! Or find them a job that values swimming. You might also want to look at your hiring practices; how did a fish get hired as a tree-climber in the first place?

When we start to realize people are doing the best they can, it can flood us with grief[12]. There's a realization that if people are doing the best they can, and I'm giving them a hard time, then holy cow, I must be the asshole! Have I ever been an asshole like that? You betcha.

Positive regard is the assumption that people are doing the best they can, with the best of intentions, at any given moment. You've probably heard versions of this in other places. It's a core belief for many programs.

"Regardless of what we discover, we understand and truly believe that everyone did the best job they could, given what they knew at the time, their skills and abilities, the resources available, and the situation at hand."

Agile Retrospective Prime Directive,
first coined by Norm Kerth[13].

"People are naturally, infinitely creative, resourceful, and whole."

- Co - Active Institute

The alternative to positive regard is negative regard. That's not really a thing but let's play with it for a moment. Negative regard would mean that you believe that people are not doing the best they can, they are lazy, and left to their own devices, they would slack off all day[14]. Maybe you do believe this. I'm not going to argue whether it's true, but I will invite you to explore it and get curious about it. Why do you imagine people are so lazy? What does this mean to your relationship with humanity? Can you lead a transformation if people are lazy slackers?

---

12 Brené Brown

13 Norm Kerth, Project Retrospectives: A Handbook for Team Review

14 This is similar to McGregor's Theory X/ Theory Y

Boundary setting is key. If you have trouble assuming positive regard, ask yourself, "What boundaries would allow me to be generous with my positive regard?" Can I put some boundaries in place that would allow people to operate in a way that doesn't cause me to view them negatively?

I find that I have a negative reaction to meandering meetings that don't have a clear objective. I created a personal boundary that I won't attend any meetings that don't have an objective stated in the invite. Of course, I can't expect people to know that I have this boundary, so if there is no stated objective, assuming positive regard, I'll ask. Think for a moment about how setting that boundary changes my impact. First, I don't have to sit in the meeting being judgy and pissy, which helps precisely no one. Second, I may have actually improved the outcome of the meeting by helping to create clarity. This supports another boundary I have: if I participate in something, I have some responsibility for the outcome.

Positive regard doesn't mean that low performance is ok. Just because you assume that people are doing the best they can, that doesn't mean that the best they can do is good enough. It can mean that the job is not for them, or maybe something is blocking them from doing better. Dig in and problem-solve with them. Are they lacking knowledge? Negative feedback won't work if they are doing the best they can.

Positive regard means that motivation is not the answer. If people are doing the best they can, motivation won't help. Looking for ways to motivate, whether intrinsic or extrinsic, is simply not the answer if the ability is not there. There is no one size fits all answer; it might be the desire that's lacking, it might be a skill, or it might be talent. I'm not detail-oriented, don't give me a job that requires attention to detail because I'll never be good at it. I might do it well for a little while if you motivate me with a piece of candy, but ultimately, it will benefit us both if someone else does this work. I don't have to feel bad about it; it's not my 'zone of genius.'[15] I have value in other areas.

Be kind to yourself. If you aren't assuming positive regard for yourself, you can't extend it to others. You can't give what you don't have. Work on yourself first. Use your self-awareness to listen to how you talk to yourself. Do you talk to yourself the way you talk to those you love? I was a little more subtle in my inner voice, I wouldn't overtly berate myself, but when I got a compliment, I would tell myself, 'they're just being nice.' Very sneaky.

Having Positive Regard for yourself and others is connected to how we show up. How you treat yourself tells people how you will treat them. When people see you being hard on yourself, they assume you will be hard on them too. Practice treating yourself kindly first.

Be gentle with yourself if you realize that you haven't been assuming positive regard. It can be hard to look into that mirror.

Overcoming it will open doors that you may not have thought possible. Hang in there; it's worth it.

Journal Exercise: Do you believe people are doing the best they can at any given moment? Explore your reactions to the question. How would it change your actions if people were doing the best they could in any given moment?

---

15 Gay Hendricks, The Big Leap.

Rapport & Empathy

Rapport

Think for a moment about someone with whom you recently had a great rapport. What was it about that person, that interaction that worked? What about someone with whom you had particularly bad rapport? What was it about that interaction that didn't work? Good rapport can feel powerful and uplifting as if anything is possible. Bad rapport can feel sticky, difficult, like pushing a rock uphill.

People who have met Bill Clinton have said that he has an uncanny ability to establish instant rapport. He starts with a humble introduction, putting out his hand and saying, "Hi, I'm Bill." As if we don't know who he is! He humbles and equalizes himself with the person he's talking with, eliminating the power differential in the first three words. Many people have commented that you feel like the only person in the room when Bill Clinton speaks to you. His gaze and his attention are steady and focused on you.

From a soul perspective, rapport happens when the frequency of our energy matches the frequency of another person. We refer to energetic frequency with everyday phrases like "they are on my wavelength," "tune into their frequency," and "find out what makes them tick." When our frequency is too narrow, we reduce the opportunity for rapport with other frequencies. I started to notice that the more I could broaden the range of my frequency, not only could I establish rapport with more people, but I could also expand the depth of the rapport with those I was already connecting with.

A friend of mine uses the metaphor of colors; when you transmit purple, people who resonate with purple will feel connected to you, but the rest won't. When you expand into blue, you start to connect with those who think and feel in blue, but you also connect more deeply with those who resonate with purple and blue. The more colors you can transmit, the more people you can connect with, and connect more deeply with each.

Listening is key for establishing rapport in your role as a Transformational Leader. That doesn't just mean listening to the 'important' people. It means listening to everyone. Deeply listening, with curiosity, looking to learn something you don't know. It's not listening for something to tie to what you already know; it's pure listening. Some call this the "beginner's mind." Listening as if you don't know what they're going to say.

When you've been around a person or group for a while, you start to see patterns. It's ok to test it out and ask if the pattern applies. It's not ok to use your experience to make assumptions and make conclusions. When you find yourself putting people and organizations in neat boxes, you know you've lost your deep listening, and you'll lose your rapport too. Some phrases to watch out for are: "This is the kind of organization that…" or "they are the kind of person who…" These are telltale signs that you are working from assumptions and extending generalizations.

A handy rapport tool was developed by the Pelican Team, specifically for establishing rapport with a client. Many of the concepts apply to rapport with anyone, including seeing the context, listening, and testing ideas before asserting them.

The Pelican Team's Rapport Process

1. LEARN the customer, the context
2. LISTEN for the need. Hear 'that's right'
3. SEEK their passion. Are they really buying in, or checking a box?
4. INTRODUCE the possible. Outcomes, not solutions. This is the first time you say something to them. Plant a seed, not a solution. Suggest what is possible, the outcomes others have gotten.
5. SEEK their approach. How would you go about it?
6. TEST the waters. Start with "Listen and pull what applies to you"
7. EXPLORE the metrics. Understand how they measure success. By this point, you get it.
8. ADAPT the solution to the environment. Adapt your approach to their context. It's now OUR solution.
9. SHARE your intent. What are you going to do for them and why? What's in it for you?
10. PRESENT your approach or solution.

You have now moved from external person to internal, you've become a trusted partner.
You must repeat these steps with each new person. Don't assume that because you have a rapport with someone's boss, that you'll have a rapport with them.

Empathy

Empathy is essential in establishing rapport because empathy tunes you into the other person's frequency. There is a lot of confusion about what empathy is, so let's clear that mess up first. This distinction blew my mind:

> *"Empathy is not about responding to an experience; it's connecting to the emotions that underpin an experience"*
>
> *- Brené Brown*

Empathy means that you feel the feelings; sympathy means that you feel sorry for the other person. Empathy is a powerful tool for rapport because you imagine how it feels to be in the other person's shoes. It doesn't mean that you can imagine their situation or agree with it; it just means you can feel how they feel. Embodying their actual emotion activates your positive regard.

I have a close friend who always complained about her brother's ex-wife; let's just call her Jane. My friend's brother was getting married and worried that Jane was going to ruin the wedding. My friend wanted to go to Jane's house and punch her in the face. Even though I didn't even know Jane, my positive regard and non-violent nature prevented me from agreeing with my friend. I tried to defend Jane, trying to get my friend to extend positive regard. What happened instead is that my friend got even more upset. She said, "Whose side are you on!? I need you on my side!" I suddenly realized that I was not showing empathy to how she was feeling. I didn't have to agree that Jane was evil. I just needed to connect with my friend's frustration. Even though I haven't been in the situation she was in with Jane; I do know what it's like to be frustrated! I had a heart-to-heart with my friend. I told her that I wasn't comfortable abandoning my value of positive regard, but I am committed to supporting her more in her feelings. She told me that she appreciates the idea of positive regard even if she can't see it in the moment of frustration. We both realized that we had been having this same friction, this same pattern of behavior in our friendship for 30+ years! We broke our old pattern and deepened our relationship. Our already long friendship found a new frequency that day.
If I apply the metaphor of tuning into my friend's 'color frequency,' you can see that initially, we were in two different colors, let's assume my friend is the color blue, and I'm purple. (the colors don't mean anything, it's a metaphor). I couldn't

hear her because I was hearing only my 'purple,' "punching this person in the face," but I wasn't tuned into the blue, "I love my brother, and I'm worried that Jane will ruin his wedding." I wasn't listening to her feelings; I was only listening to the words (purple). I don't have a brother, and I don't know Jane. But I do know what it's like to care about someone, and I do know what it's like to be frustrated (blue). Once I tuned into the frequency of her feelings, I was able to hear her and find my empathy.

When you feel like you're missing empathy, go back to our discussion about asking for help. Are you clear on how this person wants you to be with them? Do they want you just to listen, make suggestions or jump in and help them fix it? We miss the empathy boat when we make assumptions about how people want us to respond.

Empathy helps create rapport, and rapport is about connecting. As a Transformational Leader, connecting with people and connecting people with each other is the order of the day. If organizations are human systems, human connection holds the whole thing in place. The capability for human connection is at the core of any transformation.

Journal Exercise: Think about the last time someone came to you with a problem. What was your response? Did you try to solve it? Did you try to make them feel better? If you focused on the content of the problem, what would have happened if you focused on their emotion instead? Try it and see what happens.

Master your Domain: Key Takeaways

Self-Mastery is the key to authenticity. All the pieces in this section contribute to your authenticity. Authenticity isn't about adding or learning techniques; it's about peeling away all the things blocking the world from seeing the true person inside you, things that block your light from shining.

Self-mastery is a lifelong journey. The more you learn, the less you know. For me, once I started on the journey of self-mastery, it didn't mean that I stopped having emotional reactions to things, and it didn't mean that my ego didn't get in the way. It meant that I could now recognize that I was having a reaction or that my ego had taken over. At first, I couldn't realize it in the moment, and I would have to process it after it happened. I beat myself up quite a bit at first. Then I started to notice that I had a huge opportunity to make changes simply by seeing it. I began to call it out on the spot. I would say, "I feel myself having a reaction to what you're saying."

The big turning point was allowing myself to experience an emotion without having that emotion dictate my actions. When I peeled away the ego and the need to be the smartest person in the room, when I stopped trying to be intimidating, I was able to connect with human beings. All those things I was striving for were getting in the way of connecting with people.

As I was going through the peak of this journey, I was at the town pool, and one of the other moms, barely an acquaintance, saw me and hugged me. My husband said later, "Since when are you such good friends with her that she would hug you?" "Yeah," I replied, "this is my life now. People hug me all the time." I got rid of my porcupine quills, my light started to shine, and people wanted to be around me more.

Mastering your domain allows you to show up fully and lead. The practices in this section will help you become aware of the ego that can get in between you and your ability to lead. The practices will set you on a journey to continuously chip away at the armor that blocks you and slay the dragons that plague you.

"Help people see the 'we' that shows up in the 'me.'"
- Christine Cavalieri.

Mastering yourself opens the door for connection, the 'we.' Once you can show up fully, unencumbered (or less encumbered) with baggage, you are ready to step in and lead human systems.

Journal Exercise: What have you learned about yourself in this section? Where will you go deeper into your self-mastery?

Key Takeaways:

- **Self-awareness**: Notice your emotional reactions and the reactions other people have to you.
- **Emotional Literacy:** Learning to identify your emotions opens up more possibilities on what to do with them.
- **Ego:** Whatever it is, it's not about you.
- **Armor:** When you let go of your ego, you need less protection from emotional armor.
- **Deep Curiosity:** Lean into your curiosity when you get emotionally hooked or when you find yourself judging others negatively.
- **Resiliency and Recovery:** Knowing your self-worth and your values helps you stay grounded.
- **Courage:** Transformational Leaders require the courage to speak up and go against the current.
- **Showing up:** Your presence and your energy matter.

How you show up can change the outcome.

- **Asking for help:** When you ask for help, other people enroll in your success.
- **Positive Regard:** Everyone is doing the best they can in this moment.
- **Rapport:** Tune into the frequency of other people.
- **Empathy:** Empathy is not about relating to someone's situation but relating to their feelings.
- **Authenticity:** Self Mastery is what creates authenticity.

THE WE:
LEADING HUMAN SYSTEMS

After partnering in a failed startup, taking a stifling corporate job, and getting fired from another startup, I needed to pay the bills. I went back to consulting, by this point, fully focused on Business Agility. I jumped into an opportunity with a challenging and exciting client. This client had so many problems that were right in my sweet spot. I remembered how much I loved this work and why I did it in the first place. It felt good to be back. I knew how to solve their problems. But they were resistant to change. I was certified in 'Change Management,' so why couldn't I get people to do the things that would help them?

One morning before work, I was reading a Wayne Dyer book[16], and it said, "your purpose is to serve." I went into the client that day without my ego, without my armor, and just looking to be of service to the people there. The people were in pain, and I could help heal that pain. Sometimes they lashed out at me, but now suddenly, I didn't feel attacked. I felt empathy. They were being squeezed. I knew how to help, and they started listening.

I wish I could say that it all changed that day, but there was still more to learn about leading human systems.

Traditional leadership was based on the belief that we could manage people like machines. The downside of this belief is that people can be unpredictable. But the bigger issue is the missed opportunity for the upside; people can do amazing things if you let them.

A Transformational Leader's job is to "breathe life into an organization", and life implies that people are not machines. A Transformational Leader can tap into that vitality and unlock the vibrancy by creating conditions for an environment where people can thrive.

Psychological Safety

I started at a new client, and as consultants often do, we began with staff interviews to better understand the challenge. The client set us up in a small office and scheduled 30-minute interviews with key people. As we started the interviews, we noticed that the people were skittish. I assumed that there was fear in the culture, but I wasn't sure why. I found out later that the same office we used for the interviews was used a few

16 21 Days to Master Success and Inner Peace, Wayne Dyer, 2011.

months earlier to notify people of layoffs. People felt incredibly unsafe before they even entered the room.

Why is Psychological Safety so important? Tim Clark states that the conditions for innovation are "high intellectual friction and low social friction.[17]" In other words, to constructively disagree, we need trust, and we need to like each other.

Tim Clark goes on to define Psychological Safety as having four dimensions:

> *"Psychological safety is a condition in which you feel*
> *1) included,*
> *2) safe to learn,*
> *3) safe to contribute,*
> *4) safe to challenge the status quo,*
> *– all without fear of being embarrassed, marginalized, or punished in some way.[18]"*

As leaders, it's our job to create conditions for psychological safety. It's particularly important for transformational leaders to create safety because we ask people to change, and change requires an additional level of vulnerability and risk. People aren't sure they'll be competent in the new way of working; they aren't sure their skills will be valued.

If you have any hope of sparking transformation, you've got to find a way to help people feel safe to own and make change. Years and years of conditioning have created workplaces where people don't feel psychologically safe. People only do what they're told because it's even less safe not to. You may have heard threats like, "If you're not on board, you're out the door!"

17 Tim Clark, Psychological Safety, 2020.
18 Tim Clark, Psychological Safety, 2020.

Getting rid of all the people who didn't feel safe never creates safety for those who remain.

Executives are sometimes puzzled about why people feel threatened. They think of themselves as nice people, and they wonder why employees are so afraid. Finding out why people feel unsafe requires a look at the whole ecosystem. Fear is embedded. It's institutionalized. Shame has been used as a management tool for years. The system supports scarcity of rewards and abundance of punishment. Ranking people, layoffs, approvals, and 'power over' all feed into an ecosystem that can make people feel unsafe. Organizations fueled by fear end up compensating with tons of rules, regulations, and even more, fear, to try and tamp down dysfunctional behavior. It's a vicious cycle, and fear is the fuel.

Psychological Safety Myths

I hear traditional-style leaders ask questions like, "Why do people need to feel safe anyway? Is it my job to soothe people? Does everyone need a trophy?" This thinking creates a false dichotomy between effectiveness and safety. The pushback falsely equates psychological safety with coddling. Psychological safety doesn't mean that 'everybody gets a trophy,' but it does mean that when the winner gets a trophy, the rest don't get trampled on.

"Does this mean I can't tell someone when they screwed up?" Psychological safety doesn't mean the absence of accountability. It's much more effective to hold someone accountable for a screw-up when they feel safe. Safe accountability sounds like "this is screwed up"; un-safe sounds like "you are a screw-up." With psychological safety, the person can address the issue without going into a shame spiral, complaining to their co-workers, and taking time off to recover. It never feels good to screw up, but it's much easier to recover from a screw-up than it is to recover from shaming.

Shame as a Management Tool

For years, companies have used shame as a management tool. Pause for a moment and think about that. Shame as a management tool. I had an executive ask me once, "What are people so afraid of? We never fire anyone." Well, first of all, they did fire people all the time. They called them 'layoffs,' but that didn't make it any safer. My answer to the executive was, "They aren't afraid of job loss as much as they are afraid of being shamed." I saw it coming from this executive directly; when someone presented an idea or status update, they were raked over the coals and thoroughly shamed if they didn't have all the answers.

Take a close look at how ideas are discussed and evaluated in the organization. What kind of language is in use? Are ideas subject to combative conversations, or are they bandied about, played with, built on, and considered from different angles? Do objections address the idea or the person? Look for red-flag language like "And how do you plan to do that?", "We already tried that," "You haven't convinced me" vs. a more collaborative "How can we get around this limitation?" or "You're onto something, what if we …."

Helping people communicate productively and mindfully goes a long way in creating safety.

Gatekeepers

Take a look at your organization's gatekeepers. These are the people whose job is to protect an executive's time, filter ideas, and govern activity. These roles are needed to keep the organization focused. The downside with these roles is that they can spread fear, whether intentional or not.

I told a senior executive client that his organization was afraid of him. He was surprised, he asked me, "You know me, I'm not scary, am I?" I said, "No, you're not scary, but here's why everyone thinks you are." And I laid out the path to fear, using the example of Terry. Terry had information that could save the organization from a competitive threat. Her first gatekeeper was the executive's administrative assistant. Terry asked the admin to schedule time, but the calendar had the next open time six weeks from now, for 15 minutes. But this was urgent! It doesn't matter, he's busy. So, Terry accepted the time slot.

Once Terry set up that meeting, the second gatekeeper stepped in, Terry's boss. Terry's boss found out about the meeting and got nervous because Terry would be meeting with someone two levels above. The boss was worried that Terry might make him look bad. He instructed Terry on what to say, what not to say, and how to say it. In the end, the boss decides to go to the meeting just to make sure Terry doesn't say the wrong thing.

A week before the meeting, the third gatekeeper appeared, the executive's chief of staff. The chief of staff reached out to find out what Terry would say and get an advance copy of any materials. The chief of staff informs them that the executive doesn't like to hear about problems unless you have a solid solution and a proposal to get funding for it. "You can't go in there without being ready with funding, and make sure your data on the competitive threat is airtight," the chief of staff says.

When Terry mentions this meeting to her peers over lunch, one says, "oh good luck, I hear people get chewed up and spit out in there." They're not gatekeepers, but they are feeding the fears.

On the day of the meeting, the executive is running late, so the meeting time is cut in half. Terry has been advised of so many constraints she can barely speak. She waters down the message, and it sounds like this; "there may be a competitive threat; we should put some processes in place to respond if it happens." The message lacks the urgency it needs, the executive nods and asks for a follow-up with specific recommendations. Terry remains safe, but the company suffers.

Everyone is conspiring to protect themselves, which makes the executive seem scary, making Terry feel unsafe. It's now become about Terry's agenda, instead of the original goal, which was to help the company.

I hear executives tell me they are trying to better understand what's happening on the ground, but they are unwittingly blocking themselves from access to that information. When executives say, "don't bring me problems, bring me solutions!" they no longer have access to knowledge of the problems. People will now stay quiet about problems unless they have a solution. The executives have effectively closed the boundary between themselves and the intelligence in their organization.

Addressing the lack of safety in the information flow can help alleviate this. It requires the training of gatekeepers in how to manage focus while also making people feel safe and valued when they have information to share. It also requires training and coaching of people on the other side of the gate to hold their gatekeepers accountable for welcoming information in.

Layoffs

If your organization has had layoffs in the past few years, people don't feel safe. Period. Executives love to explain away layoffs, but they ignore the impact it has on psychological safety. Look at what's happening on the ground. People won't take risks. When I consult with companies with repeated layoffs, the lunch conversation inevitably focuses on what people plan to do when they lose their jobs. At a recent client, I sat down with an affable fellow named Rich and his coworker, Barb. Barb said, "I type 110 words per minute. I can get a job anywhere!" I didn't want to burst her bubble, but typing skills haven't been marketable in years. Rich asked me what certifications he should get to keep himself "marketable." All this energy and effort were understandably going into personal safety, which could instead channel into the organization's success. Ironically, they are avoiding putting focus on the things that might help prevent future layoffs.

In the wake of unavoidable layoffs, leaders need to assure people that they are safe. Any HR person will tell you this, but almost no one actually does it. It's more than a single statement that says, "we kept all you good people so that we can stay in business." It's an ongoing conversation and direction from leaders to execute on the strategy behind the layoff. Cutting costs is not compelling or safe. People feel like they're on a sinking ship. Making your remaining employees feel unsafe undermines the purpose of the cuts. If you must let people go, you want to emerge from the layoff with the strength to succeed.

Apple's strategy in 1997 is an excellent example of a layoff that emerged with strength. When Steve Jobs returned, the company was reporting losses of $1.04B. He proceeded to cut 3,000 jobs and slash 70% of the product line. His strategy was, "Our focus is spread in too many places. We need to refocus on 4 of our most promising products, create real innovation and build a strong foundation for future growth." By 1998, they reported a profit of $309M[19]. The strategy was clear; they felt like they were going somewhere, and those remaining were all in.

If you're leading a transformation in an organization that had layoffs, you've got to shift from the feeling of being on a sinking ship to the building of hope for the future. Fear of disruption does not create energy. Hope and faith in the future create psychological safety and spark energy.

Power Over

"Power Over" is the condition of one person having control over the fate of another. A simple example is a manager having power over an employee. The manager may fully control that employee's work assignment, assessment of completed work, bonus, and promotion.

As humans, we generally don't like the feeling of someone having power over us. Even when the person with power over us is benevolent, we don't like it. Why? Because when someone has power over you, you have handed your power to them. You've given up part of yourself, part of your free will, to another. At first, this may seem freeing; you have less responsibility, it seems easier just to do what you're told. You check off the boxes and get the reward; don't break the rules and avoid punishment.

Eventually, the "power over" model crumbles, causing a negative impact in two possible ways. First, people check their souls at the door. Little by little, we give away parts of our soul in order to conform to power. You hear language that sounds like, "just tell me what I need to do." The result is an organization full of people that won't think outside the box. The second

19 Steve Jobs, Walter Isaacson, 2011.

thing that can happen is rebellion. Rebellion can be explicit or very quiet and almost imperceptible. It shows up when people stop going the extra mile, stop volunteering ideas, no longer speak up, and leave the company. These impacts show up under the umbrella of 'low employee engagement,' resulting from sustained psychological damage from 'power over.'

How does your organization handle 'power over'? When people have power over other people, as happens in many organizational hierarchies, the people under power aren't safe. If two people are discussing ideas and one person can fire the other, or determine their bonus, their ideas are not equal. Even under the best conditions, a person under power is not safe.

Ultimately, we'd all love to see organizations that don't use "power over" as a management tool. If that's not a current reality for you, in the meantime, you can increase safety for those under power. One strategy is to create a leadership competency around empowerment and get specific in areas like allowing teams to pull their work assignments, peer reviews for work quality, and multi-person performance reviews. Individual competency can be rebuilt and supported for outcome-based work instead of check-the-box tasks.

Ranking

Another element damaging to psychological safety is ranking. There are stories about companies using a practice known as "rank and yank." They rank people 1...n and then fire the lowest 10% of the people. A tremendous amount of energy went into managing that process, energy they could spend developing those people. I have seen the posturing that goes on in a place like this! One executive told me that the goal was "to keep raising the bar." Keep raising the bar!? Do they think they are "even better people" out there, better than the ones they cultivated and nurtured? Even the people who retain their jobs are traumatized, left to do more with less while under threat that their job will be next to go. To protect themselves, they might undermine their peers, creating a vicious cycle of toxicity. No one feels safe in a place like that, no one.

Maybe your organization doesn't 'rank and yank,' but most organizations have some form of this in their performance review and bonus process. "Forced ranking" is the process where we rank people, calibrate their ranking across teams, so we know exactly who is better than someone else. Often there's a limit to how many people can receive a rating of "exceeds expectations." Let me just repeat that back to you, "Organizations limit how many people can exceed expectations." I'm not saying everyone has to get a trophy or even a raise, but I'd like to be in a place where there's no limit on exceeding expectations! When a company limits how many people can excel, it creates scarcity instead of abundance. Scarcity is a psychologically unsafe feeling that cultivates protective, insular behaviors instead of creative collaboration.

When we rank people against each other, it creates a zero-sum game. The only way to win is to see your peers as competition, or really, the enemy. Collaboration shuts down, and psychological safety evaporates.

Practical tools for Psychological Safety

I am often asked, "How can I make people feel safe?" The real question is, "What am I doing to make people feel unsafe?" Our job as Transformational Leaders is not to make people feel safe; it is to prevent them from feeling unsafe.

This handy SCARF®[20] tool will help you sort through what is causing a threat response in your organization. These are the things that set off a threat or reward response.

- **Status** – our relative importance to others.
- **Certainty** – our ability to predict the future.
- **Autonomy** – our sense of control over events.
- **Relatedness** – how safe we feel with others.
- **Fairness** – how fair we perceive the exchanges between people to be.

For example, getting fired can cause a threat response in 'certainty' and 'fairness.' And while 'power over' falls mainly under 'status,' it could hit multiple threat categories.

Bringing more psychological safety to an organization can release a lot of energy currently wasted in self-protection. People can channel the energy they use for self-protection into energy towards the success of the organization. Psychologically safe organizations end up being more productive and create better outcomes than those that are unsafe.

Journal Exercise: Where do you feel unsafe? Where do you see people feeling unsafe in your organization? In what ways can you impact people's safety? What do you imagine a psychologically safe organization might look like?

Diversity Equity and Inclusion (DEI)

A lot of fantastic information already exists in the space of Diversity, Equity, and Inclusion (DEI). I am not going to recreate it here. I will simply say it's not possible to be a Transformational Leader without doing your own DEI work. If you want to create

20 Your Brain at Work, David Rock.

a place where people can be psychologically safe, bring their souls to work, or be free, you'll need to learn to hold space for uncomfortable conversations. "Your job is not to control the conversation; it's to make it safe to have them."[21]

Diversity, Equity, and Inclusion doesn't simply mean that we have a diverse set of demographics on our team. It means that we extend this acceptance to a wide range of thinking and being. Transformational Leaders seek ways to uncover their blind spots and know they will screw up sometimes. When we acknowledge our screw ups, we model the behavior for others.

It's a rude awakening when we realize that our best intentions have a negative impact on others. You can't create inclusion until you are open to exploring the gaps between your impact and your intention.

A Transformational Leader's job is to breathe new life into a human system. It's not possible to have a healthy human system without diversity, equity, and inclusion.

Journal Exercise: Where do you feel resistant to the idea of diversity, equity, and inclusion (DEI)? Are there aspects of DEI that don't make sense to you? Get curious and explore where that resistance is coming from. What is the impact on the effectiveness of your leadership?

Organizational Healer

As a Transformational Leader, your soulful side is that of an Organizational Healer. Take a moment to reflect on how that feels for you. It might feel uncomfortable. I have a degree in mathematics and computer science, and an MBA; the last thing

21 Brené Brown

on my list of aspirations was soul healer. It took a long time for me to come to terms with the reality that organizations needed healing, and I can help with that. If you're uncomfortable with this too, then you are uniquely qualified to help! Why? Because you can connect with those who are uncomfortable too. You can connect the dots between the soulful and the practical.

"Our job is to hold the hope until the organization can hold it themselves."

- Kumar Dattatreyan

Phil Purrington tells a story about jumping into the pool as a kid that exemplifies the role of the Organizational Healer, to provide a temporary safety net, just until the organization gains the strength and skill to stand on its own.

> "I was about 2 ½ years old, and I wanted to jump into the pool. I was scared, but I wanted to try. So, I jumped off the side, really close to the edge, spun mid-air, and grabbed onto the side of the pool as I entered the water. My dad saw this and yelled, 'don't do that again! It's dangerous. You could hit your face on the side of the pool!' He waded out to the middle of the pool and told me to jump in, all the way in, and he'd be there to hold on to if I needed it."

Just like jumping into a pool, if we jump too close to the edge, we can cause more harm than good. Instead of saying, "See, we tried jumping, but we ended up with a bloody nose!" we can say, "we jumped all the way in, got a little water in our nose, but then we learned to swim!" That jump is hard, and it's scary. Transformational Leaders are like Phil's dad, standing out in the pool, holding the hope and faith until the organization can hold it itself.

Our job as Transformational Leaders is to make it safe for organizations to take a leap of faith. We're asking them to let go of control, step into chaos, and risk failure. Everything in the past has signaled to them that this is not safe. We're out in the water saying, "I'm here, I've got you."

Journal Exercise: In what ways does your organization need to heal? In what ways can you be the custodian of hope?

Heal the Pain

When an organization is in acute pain, you can't solve other problems, and you certainly can't build anything new. When you notice that people are resistant to your solutions, it's often because they are in pain.

Think of it this way, if you have a nail through your hand, and I come to you and say, "There are huge benefits to the mind and body through meditation. Let's do an Ohmmm." What are the chances you'll listen? What are the chances you'll punch me in the face?

Here's a little story about a time when I was a healer. It was my first day at a new job in Product Development, my first non-IT job. The VP invited me into his office for a meeting with his leadership team. On my first day, they just expected me to sit there, listen, and learn.

They quickly reviewed the status of new product launches, all of which were stuck in finance. Almost immediately, they all started complaining; "If we could only get those damn Finance people to stop being a bottleneck, we could get products to market faster. Our cash cow is in decline, and we need to replace it with something FAST! They need more people over in Finance, but they refuse to hire." There was clear, acute pain.

I will remind you; it was my literal first day in this job. Amidst the flurry of complaining, I piped in and said, "I can fix it." Silence. They all turned and looked at me. Then they laughed. They thought it was cute that the new girl was so optimistic. "It's been a problem for years, honey. We've tried everything. It's not solvable."

It was the most significant pain of a multi-billion-dollar organization, facing disruption, blocking their strategy to get new products to market. Still, they couldn't get past their own internal process. Yet, there was no energy directed toward healing this misalignment. The energy was going towards blame and finger-pointing. Everyone had dug their heels in. So, what now? Do we just let the company go out of business? The plan was for Product Development to plow ahead, building products and letting those products pile up at finance's door. The strategy was 'let it be finance's fault, not ours.'

Despite the ridicule from the leadership team, I got the go-ahead to jump in; they had nothing to lose. I found that we had 60 project managers calling ONE accountant; let's call her Jane. Like good project managers, they hounded Jane relentlessly, and they insisted Jane attend their meetings. Poor Jane was chained to her desk, attacked daily, with a stack of escalations to her boss. Jane was in pain. But no one showed any empathy for Jane. I thought that if I could heal Jane's pain, maybe I could heal the organization's pain too.

I became the goalie for Jane. I had stopped all project managers from calling Jane directly, they were to come to me, and I would prioritize the work we were to send to Jane. My Agile friends call this list a "Backlog." In Agile-speak, I was loosely playing the role of a product owner.

I got a call from my boss that evening at home. She relays that the VP called her and said, "A list!? Jardena thinks a list can solve this?! She's really missed the mark on this one."

Missed the mark. Ouch. It still stings after all these years.

What do you do with that feedback? Do you backpedal? You're new on the job, and you want to make a good impression. I'm pretty sure the list will help, but there are a lot of variables here, and I'm brand new. And now I have no safety, no air cover, no support at all. If this doesn't work, I'm screwed.

I trusted my intuition. I decided to go for it. I took a deep breath, and I said to my boss. "Let's just try it. Nothing else has worked. No one else has any ideas. You have nothing to lose." My boss relented.

Well, it worked. And lucky for me, it worked quickly. Within weeks things were moving along. Finance was happy because the pressure was off them, my VP was happy because products were launching, the relationship between the two organizations became an absolute lovefest.

"Not everything that is faced can be changed, but nothing can be changed until it is faced."
- James Baldwin

What's the moral of this story? The moral isn't the magic of making a list. The list solution wasn't perfect, and it certainly won't work in all situations. This story is about finding the acute pain, zeroing in on it, and having the courage to sit squarely in the face of pain until you can heal it. The organization had a nail in its hand, and no one was applying first-aid. I didn't know if I could solve it, but I knew it had to be solved. A Transformational Leader creates energy for the problems that *need to be solved, not the problems they can solve*. The moral of the story is that until you heal the pain, nothing else matters.

Journal Exercise: What is the most significant pain being felt by your organization right now? Is it being faced? Why or why not? What can you do to help acknowledge the pain? What would it take for you to generate energy towards healing the pain?

Create Porous Boundaries

Living systems have porous, permeable boundaries. If you think of a cell wall, it's a wall, but it lets in nutrients and information. Permeable boundaries are 2-way and exist in service to the larger organism or system. As Transformational Leaders, we do the same thing, we create clear boundaries, and we are careful not to turn the boundary into a blockade. On the flip side, we're often opening up boundaries that are already in place and may have been in place for many years.

Role Definition. The role of the Transformational Leader is the very first boundary you will define. If you read that sentence and thought, "my role was defined before I was hired," please consider that your first porous boundary. The role that was defined before you were hired; defined without your help. Now that you're in the role, you can help better define your role.

The most important thing to realize is that anything that affects the success of the transformation is in scope for your job. Stop. Let's say that again. ANYTHING that affects the success of the transformation is in the scope of your job. Go ahead. Take a moment to write a list of all the things that you have no control over, and you can't possibly be responsible for. Maybe it's the CEO's support, the vendor's liquidity, IT's priority list, the viability of the technology; whatever it is, list it out. Now put a checkmark next to all those things because they are all in the scope of your job. In the last section, we noted that a Transformational Leader creates energy for the problems that *need to be solved, not the problems they can solve*. You are responsible for all of it. I hear people worry that they'll be held accountable for something that's not possible. You may not be held accountable for the impossible, but you certainly are responsible for it. If you think this is impossible, hang in there, we'll get to that in the section on "Making Magic" and "Doing the Impossible."

Time Horizons. Time Horizon refers to the length of time for the scope of work at hand. Are we discussing a 5-year strategy or some tasks to be completed in the next two weeks? All time horizons need to work in service to each other. For example, long-term strategy informs short-term tasks, short-term tasks execute the long-term strategy.

One of the biggest causes of confusion in a transformation happens when people don't realize they are speaking in different time horizons. There are multiple time horizons in any given interaction. A technique to clarify this issue is to break the discussion into long-term and short-term, then discuss how they connect.

The slice of time horizon that's most important for a Transformational Leader is discerning between Current Reality and Future State[22].

22 Based on the work of Robert Fritz, The Path of Least Resistance for Managers.

Current Reality: Accurate description of the current state of the organization in relation to the transformation.

Future State: Describes the organization after transformation. You may have two future states, one that is several years away and another that is more near-term. Keep the organization focused on the near term.

A Transformational Leader's job is to lay the stepping stones between the current reality and future state. If you lay a stone down too far ahead, the organization won't be able to make the leap. If you don't put it far enough ahead, the organization is subject to inertia. Our job is to hold the tension between current and future.

Current reality requires a Transformational Leader to honor and acknowledge where the organization is today. It does not mean that you accept the current reality as immovable; it simply means that you know where you are. A sure way for a Transformational Leader to lose credibility is to deny the current reality. When you deny the current reality, it shuts down any action. "Why would we need to change? We're already in the future!" Be aware that your current reality as a Transformational Leader may be at odds with the future you are creating. For example, you might be getting evaluated using the exact tools you are trying to dismantle. In *Brave New Work*, Aaron Dignan coins the phrase "The Adjacent Possible." If you've ever done indoor rock climbing, you know that to reach the top of the wall, you need to find the next hold to grab onto. ('Hold' is the word for those little colorful things on a rock wall. I had to look it up.) You can't catapult all the way to the top in one giant jump.

Defining Current Reality and Future State creates organizational tension, and that tension creates energy. The energy, in turn, drives movement. Your job as a Transformational Leader is to hold this tension. You paint the picture of the future, keep that picture in everyone's head, but shift back to the current reality, and the next 'hold' people can grab onto. You are the keeper of this tension between the current and future. When it gets slack, you pull it and make it taut by redefining the future state. The Transformational Leader creates a porous boundary between current and future, with movement, but not confusion, between the two.

Share Shamelessly. Sharing shamelessly gets you a seat at every table, and *access* is essential for a transformation. A Transformational Leader needs access to traverse the organization, break down boundaries, and spread seeds for cross-pollination. If you're not at the table, you are not in the game. And why do I say "shamelessly"? Because you will share information and connections, with no regard as to whether people share back. When people refuse to share with me, I don't care; I'm sharing with them anyway. What if they take credit for my work? What if they use my work and the company gets great results? Is that fair? Yes, it's fair, because it's not about me.

A failure mode for Transformational Leaders shows up when they become insular. I have seen Leaders who won't share what they're working on until it's "ready." Human systems have porous boundaries, and information needs to flow in and out of the system. When we put a wall around the Transformation Team, it's no longer alive. It's no longer exchanging information with the organization as a whole. I notice that often Transformation teams get ruffled when local teams do something unsanctioned by the Transformation team. There's two-way learning that needs to happen. Learning can come from anywhere. When a transformation team becomes insular, they become an entity imposing upon the organization. When the organization, a human system, feels 'imposed upon,' resistance shows up. Sharing shamelessly keeps the transformation a connected part of the whole system.

An example of sharing shamelessly came to mind when someone asked for my advice because people didn't invite them to meetings they felt they should be part of. They asked me to trace it back to how I would have gotten invited. I dug deep to reflect on what I do that gets me invited to meetings.

> Here's my reflection on one example:
>
> There was a team standing up a portfolio process, it was related to my work, and I have expertise in that area. I thought I should be part of their meetings. After taking a deep breath, I realized that the first thing I had to do was let go of my attachment to being involved. I didn't need to be there, I wanted to be there, and my ego wanted to be an expert.
>
> When I shifted my perspective from my own need to theirs, I found ways to help the team improve their outcome without imposing on them. I offered the lead a new perspective, things I've seen work elsewhere. I sent an article that might help. When they opened up a little, I asked what challenges they had that I might not have seen before. I was curious about new ways they are solving problems I've encountered in the past.
>
> I started asking them for help and feedback on my work. Sharing my work opened up the dialogue both ways; now they were both teaching and learning. They could see that I cared, and it honored their effort.

> I offered to stop by their weekly meeting, share my knowledge, answer questions and leave. They started inviting me to stay for their meeting because they trusted that I wasn't there to hijack it with my agenda, but instead, I attended in service to their agenda. I got a seat at the table, but that seat wasn't for me. The team gave me a seat because I was acting in service to the organization.

I found early on that my natural curiosity about what people are working on and what challenges they are facing, worked to my advantage. I'm not an extrovert, but my curiosity sparks me to chat with the person in front of me in line at the cafeteria or in an elevator. I've noticed that C-Level executives will ask people what they are working on, so I adopted that question. I ask what their challenges are. Maybe I can help them or connect them to other people who can help them. I quickly (and somewhat accidentally) establish myself as a connector and the person who is quickly "in the know" when I walk into a client.

You'll get access when you act in service to others, and having access is one of the keys to leading a transformation. Sometimes you might be given access, but more often than not, you need to grab it. Sharing shamelessly and being curious are great ways to open up boundaries and gain the access you need.

Journal Exercise: Where are boundaries in your organization too closed? Where are they too open? Where can you alter boundaries that are no longer serving the organization?

Hold the Organization's Agenda and Identity

When you play the role of Transformational Leader, you have a unique perspective and accompanying responsibility to hold the whole organization's agenda and identity. The agenda is where the organization is going, and the identity is who the organization is. Both are important, but in most organizations, they float around in the ether. The first step is to make the agenda and identity explicit.

What does it mean to 'hold' the organization's agenda and identity? It means that you are above the fray, unbiased by the interests of any one group or person. You may have a sponsor who fits somewhere in the organization, but that sponsor has hired you to hold a purview that is larger than their own interests. I had a client once tell me that as a consultant, an outsider, I was the only one who could objectively see the whole system of their organization. Not because of my skill, but more because I had no stake in any part of the system. As an internal leader, you'll take steps to establish yourself as neutral, despite your place in the organizational structure. Holding the organization's agenda is the magical gift you hold; keep it sacred.

When you get caught in a tug-of-war between warring factions, reach for the organization's agenda and identity, and hold it up for all to see. Remind them of their own shared goals. Remind them of who they are. You won't take sides, you won't be the judge, and you can't be bought. Much like Dr. Seuss' Lorax, who spoke for the trees, you speak for the organization because the organization can't speak.

"I am the Lorax, I speak for the trees"
- Dr. Seuss

Your responsibility is to continually remind the organization of its agenda, purpose, goals, and identity and reflect back where its actions are incongruent. You don't need to scold or reprimand, and you don't even need to solve. You simply need to shine a light on the gap. You're creating a tension between the current reality and the future state. By illuminating the gap, you're creating energy that gets the team moving to resolution. What does it look like when you hold the organization's agenda? Let's start by looking at the negative; what does it look like when you *don't* hold the organization's agenda? I've seen this happen when organizations make budget cuts evenly across the board. If you truly hold the whole organization's agenda, you might invest in one area and divest in another. When budget cuts come as "haircuts," evenly distributed across the organization, it's a sign of conflict avoidance instead of doing what's best for the whole organization. As a Transformational Leader, you might simply name this, "Our strategy is to double-down on product A, but I don't see that reflected in the budget."

Another place you might hold the organization's agenda is deciding where to allocate the energy for Transformation. Are you being pulled to work with departments without considering the impact on other groups? What is driving the decision on who gets Transformation services first? When you hold the organization's agenda, you prioritize the Transformation work based on what's best for the whole organization.

Where are the organization's actions inconsistent with the organization's agenda and identity? Bringing these inconsistencies to light is a crucial activity for Transformational Leaders. Your job is to awaken the soul of the organization. You do that by reminding them of who they are and where they are going.

Journal Exercise: What is the agenda of your organization? Where do you have opportunities to uphold the agenda? Is there alignment between your organization's agenda and its identity?

Making Magic

A Transformational Leader appears to make magic by managing the energy of the organization. The term "energy" has a soulful element, but in practical terms, energy is the effort required to get things moving, to make things happen! You're getting people to take action, build excitement. You're unblocking obstacles that are keeping change from taking hold. There's practical energy applied to the work and soulful energy that catalyzes and fuels that practical energy. This is where we connect the dots between the soulful and the practical.

Our job as Transformational Leaders is to find doorways that open up to new possibilities.

To maximize productivity, organizations have traditionally kept the boundaries tight and possibilities contained. For example, the way we traditionally define job roles or narrowly define the scope of a project has limited our ability to think outside the box. You may have heard the phrase 'stay in your lane,' which discourages people from having ideas outside their job role. While boundaries are important, they can also close the doors to new possibilities available to the organization. A Transformational Leader dissolves or softens boundaries that no longer serve the organization. Making magic requires us to push those doors open and reveal what's behind them.

Once you can make magic, you are ready to do the impossible.

Journal Exercise: Think of a time when you witnessed someone do something magical at work; maybe it was something previously thought impossible, or perhaps they just had an ethereal quality about them. Now write about a time you did something magical yourself. It may not come to mind right away, start writing and see what comes up. And lastly, write about something magical that you need to do right now.

Doing the Impossible

Transformational Leaders do the impossible. Doing the impossible is a difficult thing to teach or explain. There are books filled with stories of people who do things never thought possible, but they never really explain how to do it. The process for doing the impossible is slippery, and it's hard to grab onto. If it were well-defined, no one would call it impossible.

The first step to doing the impossible is shifting from a *problem-first mindset into a possibility-first mindset.*
Problem-first mindset sees the world as a set of problems to be solved. When we're in this mindset, we seek broken things so we can fix them.
Possibility-first mindset sees the world as a whole and looks for ways to expand it.

In college, by studying computer science and math, my education was in a problem-first paradigm. Your math homework in high school was likely "a set of problems." This mindset worked well when I was debugging code but started to unravel when I tried to apply it to my sales pipeline, building wealth and even finding a husband!

The problem-first mindset explains why when business-people talk to technology people, they complain that technology people make everything seem impossible. I've heard people say, "when I talk to IT, they act like everything is such a problem!" Technology people studied math and computer science, where everything IS a problem! And we techies love it! In computer science, much of the work is troubleshooting. It's fun; it's a puzzle to solve! But the result is that we've created a problem-first mindset. The divide between IT and business teams is because technology people speak in problem-first language, and businesspeople speak in possibility-first language.

Eddie was a whip-smart client of mine with neat sandy hair and glasses, who tended to stop blinking when we got into intense discussions. Eddie's team was solving the problem of digitizing all the company's transactions, moving from scanned paper to stored data. His team proceeded to comprehensively figure out how to digitize all transaction types, including every situation that required special handling, no matter how infrequent. It was targeted to take three years. Unfortunately, there were strategic product launches this year that were dependent on digital transactions. I spoke with Eddie using a possibility-first mindset. I asked him what it would take to launch some digital transactions sooner? He told me that all transactions had to migrate simultaneously; otherwise, people would be confused about whether a transaction was digital or not. I asked him what was possible that could eliminate the constraints that were forcing them to move all the transactions over at one time. Eddie stopped blinking. Then, I watched as his eyes lit up and the skies opened, and then he started to rapidly list the simple things the team could build to make digital and non-digital transactions exist seamlessly during the transition. The team decided to build an automatic switch, so when someone clicked a transaction, the system would determine whether to open a digital or scanned paper transaction. Eddie's team launched digital transactions the next *quarter* enabling millions of dollars to pour in from the new product line. All we did was shift from a problem-first mindset to a possibility-first mindset.

Problem-solving works great for bounded problems such as a broken radio, buggy computer code, leaky plumbing. Traditional problem-solving techniques don't work for unbounded problems - world hunger, gun violence, space travel, and of course, organizational transformation. It also doesn't work so well for opportunities. When you turn an opportunity into a problem, you limit the possibilities for the opportunity.

A problem-first mindset closes off the thinking paths to new possibilities. Consider the process for troubleshooting or root cause analysis. We define a problem and then use that definition to keep the scope of the discussion and thinking constrained. By doing this, we lose the opportunity to look holistically and see the broader context. We shut down the chance to make new connections. It's amazing what doors open when you start with possibility.

Did you ever hear a process improvement person ask, "what is the problem you are trying to solve?" If you don't have a problem, many process improvement people won't even work with you. Instead, some have started asking possibility-first questions, "What is the job to be done?" or "What is the opportunity or desired outcome?" Asking the question this way expands the boundary and opens up more possibilities.

What is the difference between possible and impossible? Things are only impossible until someone does them. Think of all the things we take for granted previously thought impossible - air travel, sprinter speeds, vaccines, skyscrapers. All of these were impossible until they were possible. Transformational Leaders are the ones who pave the way to make impossible things become possible. The impossible is simply a set of possible stepping stones. Your job is not to know the entire path but to find the next stepping stone that gets closer to the goal. Standing on that stone allows people to see new possibilities and find the next stone.

What sets Transformational Leaders apart is that we have faith and confidence that even if we can't see how it can happen in the present, we know we can find a way in the future. We believe in the power of imagination. And we inspire others to do the same. We kindly lead them out of the problem-solving box. As Wayne Dyer said, "You'll see it when you believe it."

Journal Exercise: Think about a situation you are facing right now. Now instead of looking down at the problem, look up at the possibilities. If you had a magic wand, what would the situation be like? Now pick your favorite hero; Steve Jobs, Oprah Winfrey, Iron Man, Elon Musk, whoever transcends the possible in your mind. If they were in your shoes, what would they do?

Influence and Resonance

I have spent countless hours wrestling with the word "Influence." The term "influence" has a connotation of imposing ideas upon another person, bending them to your will. In no way do I wish for a Transformational Leader to convince or cajole people into agreeing with them. To get out of my wrestling match with language, I am redefining "influence" here to mean "the ability to expand someone's perspective, and spark action."

Before you can even think about being an influencer, you need to tune into the frequency of others. We discussed frequency in the section on building rapport, where we examined tuning into the frequency of another person. What would be possible if we could expand our frequency into the entire human system? From an energetic perspective, this means broadcasting and receiving multiple frequencies. From a purely practical standpoint, you already know how it feels when you walk into a tense meeting. You know how an organization 'feels' within a day of spending time there.

When you transmit from a narrow band of frequency, you only resonate with a narrow band of receivers. Transformational leaders increase their influence when they widen their band of frequency, both in transmitting and receiving.

The physics behind frequencies and resonance applies directly to organizations. "Resonance occurs when a system is able to store and easily transfer energy between two or more different storage modes (such as kinetic energy and potential energy)."[23] Resonance is not a metaphor; it is precisely how energy works in a human system. When you have a resonant frequency in music, two notes produce harmony. When two musical notes are in harmony, there is a connection between the notes, a vibration from the energy transfer. There is an amplification that happens when frequencies are resonant. You shift stored potential energy into kinetic energy. People feel energized as a result.

A Transformational Leader holds the tension between dissonance and resonance. We are creating dissonance for something old and, at the same time, creating resonance for something new. Dissonance is the disruption necessary for change, and resonance allows the change to happen. Resonance allows the influence to become smooth. When it feels hard, sticky, difficult, you don't have enough resonance yet. Ease the energy transfer and unlock latent, potential energy

23 https://en.wikipedia.org/wiki/Resonance

in the organization. You now have a transfer of energy that will spark action.

Great examples of influence and resonance are in many management ideas that have come along over the years. When a new management idea comes along, it tends to receive quick adoption when it causes a little dissonance and a lot of resonance. In practical terms, the adopted ideas are different from how we do things today, but it still fits into our current structure. There are great ideas out there that don't get adopted because organizations can't figure out where to fit them. They don't know who would champion the idea in the first place. Take, for example, the many management ideas that begin with the phrase, "have all your managers start doing…" which get quick adoption, versus those that start with the words, "have fewer managers." It's much easier to teach a skill than to remove structure.

As Transformational Leaders, our job is to increase the resonance. In the example above, finding ways to fit the new management idea into the organization will resonate more.

Journal Exercise: What is the energetic frequency of your organization? Where have you seen or created dissonance? When have you seen or created resonance? What would it feel like to hold dissonance and resonance at the same time?

Signal vs Noise

While we're on the subject of frequencies, let's get practical about signal vs. noise. The terms 'signal' and 'noise' come from radio engineering, measuring the strength of the signal, or intended sound, compared to the noise or static that makes it hard to hear the signal. As a Transformational Leader, focusing on the signal and dampening the noise is a core competency. What does this mean in practice? Dampening the noise means that you don't solve every problem that's thrown at you; you don't respond to every request. When an executive or client shares a problem with you, it is tempting to jump in and solve it. When you are fully grounded and know your self-worth, you don't need to solve everything immediately. Step back, gather more data, view the larger context, and discern between signal and noise.

I have observed people's tendency to jump in and build a solution for the first problem they hear. I had a colleague named Mark who was highly ambitious and eager to please. Mark received feedback from an executive that the transformation needed to be a set of steps they could check off. Mark proceeded to work day and night to create a presentation that forced the transformation into neat, linear boxes. While Mark was busy with that, the executive's team fell into destruction, with products losing market share and infighting within the group. As the stakes got higher, the psychological safety on the team plummeted. The team was in distress. Mark was missing all this because he gave up the connection to the team to instead work on creating steps for transformation.

Focusing on the wrong problem has two negative impacts. First, you burn time and energy on what could be the wrong problem or a presenting symptom of a more significant issue. Second, and even more insidious, is that you close off receptivity to additional signals. It's as if you have tuned your radio to static and left it there, not realizing that your favorite song is playing just a tiny turn of the dial to the left. When you focus on the noise, you amplify it, and you dampen the signal's frequency.

We don't need to ignore the noise altogether; following the noise can lead you to the signal. Noise can provide clues that reveal underlying fears and weaknesses in the process. Gently poking at the noise can open up new insights. The key is to acknowledge the noise and use it as a data point but be careful how much energy we spend reacting to it.

How do you know the difference between noise and acute pain? If someone tells you they are in pain, why aren't you applying first aid? Using the "nail in the hand" analogy, you would apply first aid by pulling out the nail before putting the bandage on. If we go back to the story from the 'Heal the Pain' chapter, the conflict between product development and finance contained a lot of noise. There was noise in the finger-pointing, the project managers calling finance to hound them, and the accusation of finance refusing to hire more people. I would have amplified the noise if I had collected a lot of data on how lousy finance was and brought it up the chain. The signal, in this case, was that the priority of work was unclear. The even bigger signal was that the organization culturally chose to solve the problems they could control and not put energy into the significant issues outside their control. The acute pain was that products were not getting out to customers. By looking for the signal driving the acute pain, we can home in on it and cut through the noise.

Let's get back to my eager colleague Mark. Mark thought he could ingratiate himself with the executive by responding to the linear, stepwise transformation request. Instead, he shut off his connection to the team and closed off the possibility of solving it. By using the noise as a clue, Mark might have asked the executive, "what is important about a stepwise process?" Attachment to the need for a stepwise process revealed a fear of uncertainty, which turned out to be the very thing that was holding this organization back.

The Lean techniques of "the five whys" or the Ishikawa, or fishbone diagram, are great tools to start peeling back noise that presents itself as a signal. Two words of caution on these tools, they are only a starting place. First, be careful not to ignore acute pain when you have found the root cause. Second, sole reliance on these tools will limit you to "what exists" and block the creativity of "what could be." As with all tools, use them to gain insights, but don't become dependent on them.

Practice tuning into the true signals in an organization and dampening the noise. When tempted to solve a problem, take a moment to explore whether the problem is signal or noise.

Journal Exercise: What problems were you presented with this week? What work requests came your way? Reflect on your reaction. Where could you have looked deeper to find the true signal?

Sparking Action

"A good leader allows leadership to be taken."
- Sally Parker

From the soulful to the practical, you are responsible for sparking action. Soulfully you are managing the energy of the system, and you are inspiring people. Practically, you use tools and mechanisms to spark that energy in very tangible ways. Remember, our definition of leadership was taking responsibility for changing your world. The more people you can get stepping into leadership, the more momentum you will enable.

Transformation is undoubtedly about mindset, but unless people take action, it will be impossible to tell. Your job is not to force people to take action, not with a checklist, not with motivators, not with fear. Your job is to unleash the latent energy, the energy that is already there and being squandered. Entropy is the measure of the amount of energy in a system that is unavailable to do work. Most organizations have a lot of entropy; that energy is available and waiting for you to convert it into productive energy.

"The key to leading effectively is knowing the things that make up your environment and then helping to arrange them so that their power becomes available."

- Sun Tzu, The Art of War

A great tool for sparking action is to create tension between the current reality and future state[24]. When you can clearly communicate the organization's current state and what the future looks like in a way that resonates, it creates kinetic energy, and people feel a pull towards the future. It's a little like magic, but even magic requires work. First, you need to help people understand their part in moving to the future. Tying back to our discussion on time horizons, it helps to show them what time horizon they are operating in. You'll also add in an element of tangibility, making it real.

For example, suppose our current reality is product-focused, and we want our future state to be more customer-focused. That sounds great, but if I drive a delivery truck, I have no idea what I will do differently. As a Transformational Leader, you might paint a picture that delivery truck drivers are customer touchpoints, with an opportunity to get real-time customer feedback. We want to experiment with delivery truck drivers exchanging more information with the customer in the future. As a Transformational Leader, you don't need to outline the

24 Based on The Path of Least Resistance for Managers, Robert Fritz.

change to each person, but you need enough tangibility for it to spark action. Otherwise, it's another meaningless list of "areas of strategic focus."

When you start to make progress, the tension between the current and future will loosen. There's less urgency because the metrics have improved, and people feel better, less frustrated; our revenue is growing, the boss has stopped yelling. Now is the time to readjust your future state. Your role is to keep that tension. Conventional leadership language for this was "create urgency" or "light a fire." I dislike this language because it smacks of manipulation. This kind of language raises a threat response in our brains. When leaders would share successful quarterly numbers, they always felt compelled, in the same breath, to remind everyone that they still had work to do. I find it insulting, as if they thought we were all going to play ping pong all day. I would hear leaders say things like, "we doubled our revenue, but we still need to double it again!" which feels hard and frustrating. Instead, try something like, "All of your hard work has opened up new opportunities and possibilities, which we can leverage to double our revenue next quarter. We tapped into new markets last quarter. In the coming quarter, we can learn more about these new customers and expand into the market." Build on the success in a tangible way, instead of just continuous pushing.

The truck driver who now gets feedback from his deliveries experiences renewed energy in his work. He's no longer a machine, sent to drop off boxes, but part of the living ecosystem, connecting with customers. His demeanor changes, and he may start looking forward to seeing his customers. He also feels more connected to the company's identity because he has moved from being an end-node delivering product to being part of the feedback loop back to the company.

Journal Exercise: Where is your transformation lacking energy? How can you use current and future states to spark action?

Resonant Communication

If it's a standard competency for a Transformational Leader to communicate clearly and compellingly, why is it so rare to see in practice? Let's look at what gets in the way of resonant communication in Transformational Leaders, what we can do to get buy-in and bring people along, and finally, how we can do all this while disrupting the status quo.

In the prior section, we discussed that when you transmit from a narrow band of frequency, you only resonate with a narrow band of receivers. Think about your communication. Where can you increase your frequency band? One way to do this is by including head (thinking), heart (feeling), and gut (intuition) language in your communication. Different people resonate with different origins of ideas, and by touching on all three, you increase your frequency band. For example, you can connect the head, heart, and gut by saying, "Something is telling me that we're missing a customer segment; the focus groups from young people don't feel as enthusiastic as the others. I pulled the ad data and compared it to the other groups; millennials have a very low click-through rate." This example starts with intuition, moves through the heart and into the head. The sequence is flexible. You might instead say, "I am looking at the data, and something doesn't feel right. I sense that we're missing something."

A Transformational Leader creates clarity where there is chaos. Michelle Obama wrote the following describing her husband, Barak; "His job, it seemed, was to take the chaos and metabolize it somehow into calm leadership-every day of the week, every week of the year."[25]

To create clarity, you'll need to make sense of chaos and shed the things blocking your message.

Shed for Resonance. Resonant communication comes from shedding the things that are blocking your frequency from shining through. As a human being, you are born with the ability to communicate and connect with other humans. We often look to 'build' skills to improve our communication. And while we can all learn communication skills, most communication problems are in the 'stuff' that gets between the speaker and the listener. What stuff? Worrying about how you sound, concern with how you look, fretting about how you're perceived, what people will think, the list goes on. Peel away those layers, and all people will hear is what you're saying. When we hear people speak this way, we describe them as "authentic," and it's like you have a direct line to precisely what they are saying, without anything blocking it. You can't learn to be authentic; you already are. Just let people see it.

Zealotism. True confessions, I've been guilty of being a zealot. Have you ever worked with someone so fanatical about a framework that they seemed oblivious to reason? They got upset whenever anyone tried to question the framework or process? Did it almost seem like they were brainwashed? They view the world as people who "get it" and people who "don't get it."

> ***Zealot:*** *a person who is fanatical and uncompromising in pursuit of their religious, political, or other ideals.*

Zealots have seen the light, and they think everyone else should see it instantly too. Did I mention I can be like that

25 Becoming, Michelle Obama, 2018.

sometimes too? I think we all have a little zealotism in us. When I first learned about the benefit of developing people with T-shaped skills, I tried to force it on everyone. *T-shaped skills* mean that people develop deep expertise in one area while also developing broad knowledge across other areas. Developing people this way allows an organization to adapt their skill sets as the needs ebb and flow. The problem is that not all skills are available to everyone. I found this out when I tried to push T-shaped skills on a marketing team; they laughed and told me that copywriters couldn't do artwork and vice versa. They were right; I was a zealot. We worked together to find other ways to create resilience in the team, but developing T-shaped skills was not the right answer for them.

A lot of us get into the Transformation space because we are true believers. As true believers, we feel so moved by the possibilities that sometimes we can't see what it was like before we believed. We suffer the peril of the newly converted. It can be frustrating to look back and wonder why people aren't moving as quickly as you did. If you want to make a difference, you'll have to bring them along.

A big failure mode in working with executives is showing up like a zealot, like an evangelist sent to save the organization from the end of the world. It turns people off immediately-especially executives.

Zealots lose credibility. If you are brainwashed, people feel they can't trust you. They don't know if you are preaching the gospel or trying to help solve their business problem. Are you weighing all options? Are you able to look at things objectively? When you are seen as a zealot, people can't be sure. Even when they 'get it,' no one wants a zealot to implement it. Executives know that a zealot can't bring people along; they can't operationalize the change.

Zealots are emotionally charged. Passion is a beautiful thing. I am passionate about making workplaces more humane. But sometimes, that passion can block listening and empathy. I encourage people to allow for emotion in the workplace. Emotions are a great source of information, but when someone is so emotional that you can't reason with them, they aren't collaborative, and they lose their power.

Carol Dweck's work on growth vs. fixed mindset[26] has gained popularity in the transformation space. I have never witnessed anyone who learned this concept and said, "Hey, that's me! I have a fixed mindset!" But ironically, many of us have a fixed mindset about changing mindsets. Zealots have a fixed mindset, "This transformation is great, and if you don't get it, you are stupid." No one says those words, of course, but it's implied.

Your audience has likely been running a successful business for years. It doesn't play well when you come in to tell them they are doing it all wrong. Look for specific challenges that you can help with and start there.

As a leader, be aware of when you may inadvertently create zealots and make sure you give people the tools to channel their passion productively. A client of mine got very excited about the possibility of transformation. They were so passionate that they alienated the entire department. I initially failed to teach them how to bring others along, so we backtracked, and I helped them by using many of the tools in this book.

Journal Exercise: Take a moment to reflect in your journal about how your passion is impacting others. Is it inclusive and inviting or is it exclusive and imposing? How can you make a shift into a more inviting space?

26 https://www.ted.com/speakers/carol_dweck

Getting Buy-In (hint: don't ask for Buy-In)

Probably the most frequently asked question I get from Transformational Leaders is "How do I get buy-in?" Here's some cold, hard truth for you: as soon as you ask for buy-in, you've given away your power. By saying that you require support, you've set yourself up as a dependent, someone who needs something. Do you know how draining it is for an executive to spend their day listening to people who want something from them? Wouldn't it be refreshing if you showed up offering them something?

A CIO client who was been hesitant to start an Agile transformation because he didn't want to risk a major product launch. My predecessor had asked for support, pitching the wonderful collaboration and faster delivery times of Agile. I didn't ask for support. I explained how we could start by de-risking the launch, using shorter feedback loops, and solving the riskiest technology issues first. No big training rollout, and no disruptive restructuring, just simply inserting shorter cycles so he could know sooner when something was at risk. And we'd make sure to work on the riskiest items first, so we reduce the risk early. The buy-in was instantaneous. In the chapter on "Doing the Impossible" I talked about finding the next adjacent possible stepping stone. Buy-in is also about finding that next stepping stone. I didn't get carte blanche on day-one, I earned it one step at a time.

Frame the discussion as "you (executives/company) have a need, here's how I can help you." Walk-in with the assumption that the executives want to hear what you have to say. It's a power position. They need you. The moment you go in begging and asking permission for 'your idea', you've given away your power. Remember, you were hired for this role, start with the assumption they want you to do it.

To be super-clear, taking a power position does not mean that you become arrogant, condescending or belligerent in any way. Don't snort the ultimatum "do you want my help or not?" It's also not a test to see whether they are worthy of your help. Everyone, every organization, is worthy of your help. You fully understand that this is how the game has always been played, and you are gently guiding the game in a different direction. You're not giving in to power and you're not wielding power over. You are in service to the organization.

Journal Exercise: Whose support is key but missing, for you to successfully help the organization? What is important to those key supporters? Why haven't they given support? How might you connect your work to the outcomes that are important to them?

Executive Communication

I have been a witness to many pitches given to executives that went wrong. In a conference room nestled so deep in the inner sanctum of the C-Suite, that it didn't even have a room number, I watched a presenter named Jim walk in to make his pitch. Jim was visibly nervous, holding a thick deck of slides. Jim proceeded to drone on about his team's research and their findings, apologizing for the dense slides the whole time. The executives listened for about 2-3 minutes before interrupting and asking about the conclusion. When an executive questioned Jim's approach, he backpedaled and offered to change course. The executives thanked him, and he left. Jim reported back to his team and peers that the executives have short attention spans, but they liked the content. Jim has a complete misunderstanding of what just happened.

The first mistake Jim made was that he didn't talk to executives like an equal. It's hard, I know. There's a ton of pressure when you go into an executive meeting. Speaking in a conversational tone helps establish a human connection. Review the section on establishing rapport for tips. You need to be able to interrupt and push back respectfully. When questioned, Jim folded immediately. There was no reason to back down; all he had to do was explain his reasoning. Be direct and honest. I hope this goes without saying, but this doesn't mean insulting, shaming, or using condescending language. Don't be stiff. I mean it, don't be stiff. Don't memorize and recite your pitch. Practice and know it, but it cannot sound like a 5th-grade book report.

Wait, isn't it risky for Jim to disagree with a higher-up? As an exec, if I invest in you and trust you, I need to know that you will steer me right. If you are bending to pressure, I can't feel confident that you'll stand up to me or others who exert pressure on you. When you stand firm, it makes me feel like you are grounded in the company's best interest. When you are truly holding the organization's agenda, disagreeing is in service to the whole organization. Work on countering with the facts, not the person. Making the executive, or anyone, feel stupid is probably not your best path, but expanding their perspective will shift the trajectory. And remember, a shift in perspective doesn't always happen on the spot. Someone might disagree now, think about it, and come back later with a different opinion.

Jim made the mistake of lacking brevity. Brevity is key. Work on your language so that it's crisp and concise. The classic 'elevator pitch' is a great exercise to hone your message. While your peers have more tolerance for circuitous discussion, you need to get to the point with executives. I've heard people say, "executives have attention-deficit disorder." Please don't say that, and please don't even think it. Executives have tremendous focus; executives don't have time to wait for you to get to the point, so get to it quickly. An executive's job responsibility is broad and shallow; yours may be narrower and deeper. Let's give them some credit and honor their perspective.

Here are three tools to help you be concise. First, start with your conclusion. Executive presentations are not a mystery novel where you take them through your whole journey. Start with the end. You can create openness in their minds by stating the question you will answer and then giving your answer. Starting with the question gets their mind in curiosity mode before you provide them with the conclusion. For example, "We asked ourselves why the over 65 group was our weakest market. We found out that it's because the font on the website is too small."

The second tool for conciseness is to state a conclusion and let them ask for more detail or ask if they would like more background. You will lose the listener in all the details if they're not ready to hear them. When they ask for more information, their brains are engaged. The third tool is to prepare soundbites. Get the language for your essential points just right so that you can make an impact in a few words. You don't need to memorize everything you're going to say, but you will need to develop a few key phrases that deliver a punch.

According to Stephen Krempl,[27] you should make sure you can answer the following three questions executives ask. If you can answer them before they ask, you'll establish instant rapport.

27 Stephen Krempl: www.WinningintheWorkWorld.com

1. How much will it cost?
2. Who else has done it?
3. Can you do it?

Be clear about how you want their support to look. Have a clear intention of what you want the outcome to be. What do you need? Is it budget? Is it vocal support? Do you need their time? If you don't ask for what you need, you'll just get a head nod.

The POWER Start[28]: An Executive Communication Tool.
The acronym POWER stands for:

- Purpose - why are you there?
- Outcome - what is the outcome you envision?
- What's in it for me (WIIFM) - why do they care?
- Engagement - what does it look like ongoing?
- Roles and Responsibilities - what role do you need them to play? What responsibilities are you asking them to take on?

When communicating with executives, be yourself, establish rapport while being clear and concise. Start with your conclusions and focus on the outcomes. Be clear on what you are asking from them and what they'll get out of it.

Journal Exercise: What is your core message to executives? Does your message uphold the organization's agenda? What do you need to let go of to stand in your power without your ego taking over?

28 POWER Start: Credit Agile Coaching Institute

Love your Boss (or Client)

We're all living in the space of current reality, and often having one boss that determines your fate is our current reality. It's not ideal, and I hope your Transformation work will change that, but for right now, the reality is, you probably have a boss (or a client).

It is common for the 'boss' of a Transformational Leader to be old school. Sometimes it's two levels up, but it's there. The world doesn't change in an orderly fashion. So how do we implement new ways of working while being directed in old ways? For starters, you need to love your boss. That old-school, rigid person who seems to be working against you? Yup them.

For the few years between leaving my company and getting back into consulting, I took a job as an employee at a large company. The company was very command and control. I had a boss who was old school. They hired me, in part, to bring Agile to the organization, but more as an Agile ambassador while I did other work. My boss wanted to check the Transformation box on their performance agreement, but they didn't know what they were really asking for. I got myself into trouble on a regular basis. I tried to get feedback on slides before they were perfect. I ignored assignments and worked on things I thought were more important. My boss yelled at me... a lot.

Have you been in a situation where your boss asked you to do something transformational, but they didn't really understand what they were asking for? Maybe they wanted the benefits of change but were not willing to give up control. Speed up responsiveness but not give up the approval process? Get stuff done faster, but not prioritize? Or worse yet, maybe your boss is toxic. Maybe your boss is sowing seeds of distrust amongst the team. Or perhaps they are stealing your ideas. Are they blocking your access to their boss? This stuff really happens!

How can you run a transformation with a boss like this? No one would blame you if you left to find a place where they are 'ready.' But as Christopher Avery says, "Will you only transform organizations that don't need transformation?"

When I say "love your boss";
Do I mean "get to a place where you can deal with your boss?"
... No
Do I mean "work around your boss?" Like a clandestine agent?
...No.
Do I mean "kiss your boss' ass?"
... Super-No!

By love, I mean extending positive regard. Assume they are doing the best they can in this moment—empathy, appreciation, and understanding. Like you might view a young child because when it comes to new ways of working, like a child, they haven't learned it yet. They are not immature in all ways, just in this way. They may be earlier on the learning curve than you are and less mature than you want them to be in this specific way. Your job is to bring them along.

What did I do with the old school boss that yelled at me a lot? I stayed calm. I kept a sense of humor. I started to inject small nuggets of education while I met them where they were. I found out what was important to my boss. I found their acute pain and worked on healing it. I gained trust by finding ways to love them. And I kept finding opportunities where I could push.

That boss today? A huge advocate of Agile Transformations.

They were never a bad person; they just didn't know any other way to operate. The old school way had brought them success in the past. And if no one is willing to teach the people who don't know, how will they ever understand? They were a product of a toxic system; they were passing along the pain. You can help them heal their pain.

Journal Exercise: Get curious about your boss/client. Is there a fear causing them to behave in a way that's causing you difficulty? What is underneath your difficulty with their response?

Truth-Teller and Trusted Advisor

Truth-Teller. A Transformational Leader often plays the role of Truth-Teller. Your role is like that of a mirror, reflecting the truth of the human system back to itself. A truth-teller is direct and honest, without judgment. The skill lies in finesse. The secret is frequency and resonance. We've discussed this in prior sections; let's apply it here.

As truth-tellers, we give voice to the unsaid. What is the frequency in the room or the organization? What is no one saying? When you give voice to something that's already there, it matches the existing frequency. It might shock people that you said it out loud, but it lands. And sometimes, you'll be wrong. It helps to frame it as a question like this, "I'm sensing that there's a hesitancy here, am I right?" As truth-tellers, we say what needs to be said, it comes through us, but it's not about us.

I recently worked with a team that was part of a Business Agility Transformation. They were trying so hard to do the right thing, but I could just sense that Agility wasn't resonating with the nature of their work. I asked them, "does this make any sense for your work?" They sheepishly admitted that they didn't think so. I went to the department head and asked what she thought. She agreed, the approach we were using didn't fit their work, and there wasn't a real need to improve that team anyway. Their customers were pleased, and we had bigger opportunities for improvement in other areas. I can find a way to leverage Agility to improve any team if I try hard enough, but the truth was, I needed to let this team off the hook. We allowed them to adopt the Agile practices they felt would help them, at their own pace.

Keep in mind, truth-telling is a role. You are not always playing that role. While you should always be truthful, the specific role of reflecting the system back to itself is not constantly on. That doesn't mean you are lying when you're not in the truth-telling role. It just means that hearing constant jarring truths can be exhausting. Choose wisely, speak up when the truth is already in the air, it will be of service to the group, and the group is ready to hear it.

When you are in the role of truth-telling, it is important to be precise with your language. Name what you see and feel, don't add judgment or evaluation. For example, rather than saying, "Everyone clammed up because you are battle-scarred over budget cuts, and everyone wants to protect their turf." Try a more fact-based inquiry, "I think I just felt everyone clam up. Why do you think this is happening?" If you don't get movement, you might move into a probing question like, "Is it because you are protecting your team from future budget cuts?"

Playing the role of truth-teller can unlock new possibilities for an organization. You are building a relationship between the organization and the truth. By modeling what truth-telling looks and sounds like, you create the organizational capacity of courage to speak the truth and the savvy to say it in a way that people can hear.

Trusted Advisor. Another role you play as a Transformational Leader is that of a trusted advisor. A trusted advisor is someone that is pulled in for guidance and advice. It's important to remember that in a Transformation, most people's priority is their day job. As a Transformational Leader, it is your job to help make connections between their day job and new ways of working. I've led Agile Transformations where there was rigid compartmentalization between Agile and "other problems." I would get shooed away with the comment, "this isn't about Agile." It was my job to get back in there and connect the dots. Otherwise, we would end up with a box of Agile and a totally fragmented transformation.

Here's the paradox. You can't appoint yourself a trusted advisor, and no one will give you the role, yet without it, you will fail. It's like the riddle of the sphinx. Go check out the section on sharing shamelessly, building rapport, and tuning resonant communication. Everything in this book leads you to the natural conclusion of being a trusted advisor.

Note: I'm using the term "Trusted Advisor" intentionally instead of the currently popular term "coach." You may do some coaching, but you are giving advice; you are giving your opinion. In my eyes, the term 'coach' in the context of organizational transformation doesn't connote enough backbone. You should absolutely use coaching techniques situationally. In my view, a coach sits outside the game while a Trusted Advisor is in the game. Transformational leaders are in the game.

Journal Exercise: What truths need a voice in your current environment? Jot down some ways you might voice those truths without blame or judgment. Perhaps try starting with "I'm noticing that…." or "I've observed…"

Let it Be Messy

"Don't judge the process; judge the outcomes."

Transformations are messy. If you allow a transformation to be judged by how it looks or feels, it will be shut down. Your role is to keep the organization focused on what's really happening and the outcome. One way to do this is by helping people interpret the meaning behind what they are seeing and feeling.

I'm going to start with a metaphor in nature, and then we'll take a look at a human system and finally a real-world business example. We're dancing between spirit and practice again. Hold my hand.

There's an old story about a caterpillar[29] and the lessons of the messy struggle.

> One day a boy was playing outside, and he found a caterpillar sitting on a branch near his home. Fascinated by the caterpillar, he put it in a large jar with holes in the top, named him Buddy, and gave him new food every day.
>
> One day the caterpillar started building a cocoon, just as the boy had learned in school! Finally, a small hole appeared, and the butterfly started to struggle to come out. The boy was concerned. The butterfly was struggling so hard to get out! It looked like Buddy wasn't making any progress breaking free!

29 Based on the story attributed to Sonaira D'Avila via Paulo Coelho's blog

> The boy had to help, so he got his scissors and snipped the cocoon to make the hole bigger. The butterfly quickly emerged! But it had a swollen body and small, shriveled wings. The boy waited for the wings to unfurl, but they never did. The butterfly was never able to fly.
>
> The boy didn't understand what had gone wrong.
>
> The next day in school, he learned that the butterfly's struggle to push its way through the tiny opening of the cocoon pushes the fluid out of its body and into its wings. Without the struggle, the butterfly would never, ever fly. The boy's good intentions hurt the butterfly.

In living systems, struggle gives shape to what is possible. Organizations learn through struggle. It is not your job to ease the pain of transformation. It is not your job to make it clean and neat. Create conditions for transformation and allow the organization to learn.

Self-Organization. A self-organizing group of people has a shared goal, with some constraints, and figures out how to get it done. The "what" may be dictated, but the "how" is determined and managed by the group. On a small scale, Agile teams use self-organization when the product owner gives a requirement (or user story) telling the team the 'what' and the 'why.' A requirement might state: "As a customer, I want the website to automatically fill in my name and address so that I don't have to type it in every time I place an order." The team then figures out how to make this happen and weighs the possible implementation options. As Transformational Leaders, we help the organization self-organize in a larger context.

There are several exercises I use with teams to illustrate this. Here's one that I first saw demonstrated by Michelle Sliger.

> Part 1: This works best with a minimum of about 30 people; more is even better. I ask everyone to line up against the wall. I ask for a volunteer to be the manager. I ask this person to line everyone up by last name. People can help the manager but can't talk to each other. (People naturally want to self-organize.) I set a stopwatch. The manager is typically very organized, using some rudimentary sorting algorithm. It's quiet, and it's orderly. Depending on the size of the group and how well they know each other's names, it usually takes around 5 minutes. I thank the manager and ask them to place themselves with the group.
>
> Part 2: I ask the group to line themselves up by birthday, month, and day (not year!), I point to one end of the room and say, "January down there!". Then I yell, "GO!" It gets loud, people bump into each other. There is mass confusion. People are laughing. People find ways to blast out their month, yelling things like "April over here!" Things settle down as people find their places, and I announce the time. It seems no matter how large the group is, it takes around 25-30 seconds.

I ask the group, what if a bigwig had walked during part 1? What would they say? The answers are usually along the lines of "Good job!" and "I can see progress here." What about if the bigwig walks it during part 2? "We might get fired."

The lesson is that just because it looks messy and chaotic doesn't mean it's ineffective. Don't let orderliness be your metric. We'll talk more in the next section about emergence, but for now, let's just notice how orderliness is not an accurate measurement of success.

Messy but Effective. I can hear you thinking, "Enough about butterflies and lining people up. Those stories are cute, but my company doesn't make butterflies or line people up by birthday." I promised you a final story about how this shows up in real life.

> I was leading an Agile Transformation of 2500 people, most of whom were resistant to change at least partially due to a fear-based culture stoked by frequent layoffs. Leaders said they wanted to be Agile and then regularly undermined the Agile Coaches. They wouldn't follow the actual Agile Scrum practices. I lost many Agile Coaches who said the company "wasn't ready" and "a mess." There's a popular mantra in the Agile community that we "meet people where they are," but it's easier said than done. In this case, this is where they were, they were in a painful mess, so I met them there.
>
> I asked teams to do one thing: find ways to re-organize their work so they could deliver value sooner. I let them throw the rest of the Agile practices out the window if they wanted to. I tipped the sacred cow of Agile. More coaches quit, and my Agile community colleagues were horrified.
> The Transformation was messy. The metrics for how many teams were following Agile practices were abysmal. The reports going up to senior executives

> said, "get rid of this Agile thing; it's not working." Then something happened. The department met its yearly financial goal in only six months. Wait what?!? "Check those numbers!" demanded the executives. "How can this be?" The finance team checked the numbers and found that it was understated. We had actually exceeded the yearly goal two months earlier.

I tell this story to drive home the point that messy doesn't mean bad. The criteria of a successful transformation aren't whether it feels the way people expect it to feel or looks the way people expect it to look. It's not going to. It's going to look and feel different, and if you judge it against old paradigms and old metrics, you won't break through the proverbial cocoon.

Foolish Consistency. When working on transformations, I often have people insist that things should be consistent; all teams should use the same process; i.e., Scrum by the book. When I ask "why?" there isn't a real answer. It goes like this:

"Why is consistency important here?"
"Because otherwise people will be confused."
"Confused how?"
"Well, they won't know what to do when they join a new team."
"Presumably, they don't know a lot of things when they join a new team. Could this be part of the onboarding?"
"Well, we won't be able to measure agility across teams."
"We can measure outcomes."
"The boss likes consistency."

> *"A foolish consistency is the hobgoblin of small minds"*
> *- Ralph Waldo Emerson*

Consistency is a trade-off question. Often, we assume consistency is unquestionably good. In reality, consistency is situational, sometimes there's a benefit to consistency, and sometimes there's more benefit to autonomy. A classic example is software procurement. I've seen companies who limit teams to a list of software packages. They can't use software that's not on the list without a lengthy application process. There are benefits to centralized procurement; the company can negotiate better prices, IT can ensure that the software is secure, people can communicate easily across teams. But what about the team that needs to respond quickly to market changes and has to wait to get the software they need? Are you willing to give up a multi-million-dollar market opportunity to save a few thousand dollars on software licenses?

What about a team trying to market in a new channel and can't get access to the tools for that new channel? And even more significant, what about a team that is told they are empowered but feels frustrated and disempowered by not being able to get the software they need? The disempowering of teams may be the most significant trade-off consideration for loosening consistency. The simple solution is boundaries. Where does lack of consistency cross a boundary? Create a boundary, such as "Buy any software you want after you've seriously considered the benefits of what we already have and cleared it with the security team."

Question the assumptions behind the need for consistency. There is a natural tension between order and disorder. You can hold that tension by allowing for messiness in service to the outcome and allowing orderliness to hold space for the messy. Look for specific ways to support the real value of consistency and let go of the attachment to have it look neat.

Journal Exercise: Where is the need for orderliness holding back your transformation? What is the deeper fear behind being messy? What would be possible if you helped the organization let go of the need for orderliness?

Leading Human Systems: Key Takeaways

I had started my career not wanting to deal with people, and here I was, leading human systems. What I found was that nothing worthwhile can happen without people. It is truly rewarding to observe psychologically safe spaces that I've helped create, where I can see people working through conflict in a healthy way and watching people step up and take leadership. Creating conditions and cultivating a thriving human system is exponentially more effective than fixing a problem.

Journal Exercise: What have you learned about your own leadership and how you lead human systems? What areas of leadership will you continue to develop your own capability?

Key Takeaways:

- **Psychological Safety:** Creating psychological safety is a precondition for transformation.
- **Diversity, Equity, and Inclusion:** Transformational Leaders do their own internal DEI work and educate themselves on systemic marginalization.
- **Organizational Healer:** Hold the hope of transformation until the organization can hold it itself.
- **Heal the Pain:** No change is possible when there is acute pain (or a nail in your hand). Apply first aid before transformation.
- **Create Porous Boundaries:** Soften boundaries to allow information to flow freely through the

organization. Start by sharing shamelessly.

- **Hold the Organization's Agenda and Identity:** Transformational Leaders hold up a mirror to remind the organization of where they're going and who they are.
- **Making Magic:** Re-vitalize the organization's energy, inspire people by opening up new possibilities.
- **Doing the Impossible:** Move from a problem-first mindset into a possibility-first mindset.
- **Influence and Resonance:** Create energy by unlocking latent, potential energy to kinetic energy in the organization. Hold the tension between dissonance and resonance.
- **Signal vs. Noise:** Don't react to noise; seek the signal. When you jump too quickly to the noise, you turn off your reception to other signals.
- **Sparking Action:** Leaders create action when there's a tension between current reality and future state. Enabling others to lead creates momentum.
- **Resonant communication:** Communicate with resonance by peeling away anything that blocks your authenticity. Be mindful of becoming a zealot.
- **Getting Buy-In:** Don't ask for buy-in.
- **Executive Communication:** Start with the conclusion, be concise, and focus on how you can help the organization.
- **Love your Boss (or Client):** Extend positive regard, help heal their pain and keep pushing.
- **Truth-teller and Trusted Advisor:** Be direct and honest, without judgment, giving voice to the unsaid. Don't be afraid to give advice.
- **Let it Be Messy:** Just because something is messy doesn't mean it's not effective.

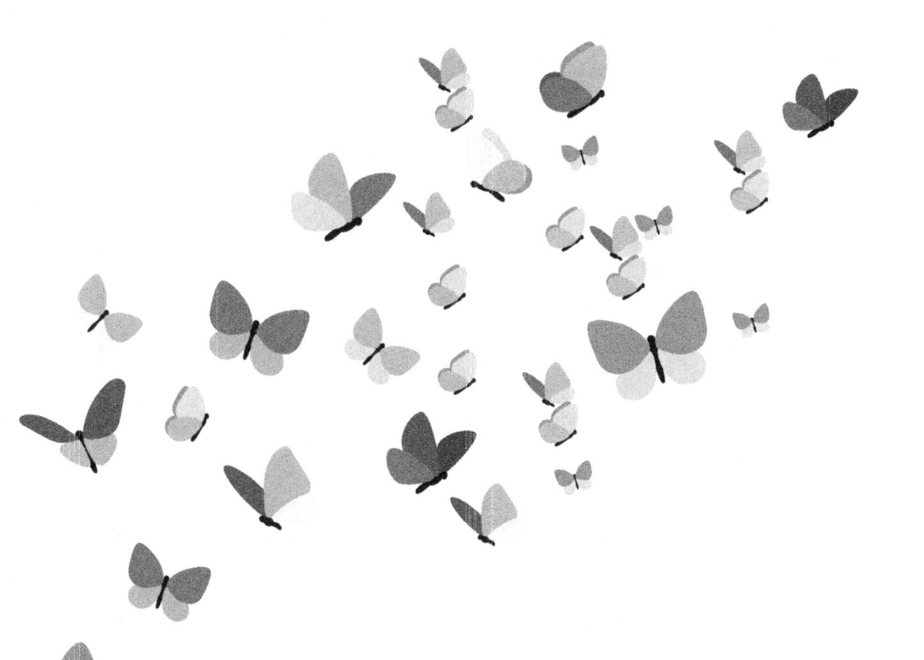

THE SYSTEM: ORGANIZING FOR ADAPTABILITY

By this point, you have a basic understanding of how to manage yourself in the role of Transformational Leader, and you know how to lead others through a transformation. Now let's delve into how to expand that into the larger organizational system.

When I had my first job out of college, I noticed that the programmers, who had been the elite minds in college, were now the dregs of society in the corporate world. These brilliant minds couldn't seem to deliver anything on time, and when they finally finished, it rarely worked properly. As

I worked through trying to solve that problem, I started with the programmers. I tried to teach them better debugging skills and coding guidelines, and I even wrote a code generator to save programming time. But it wasn't a problem with the competency of the programmers. The problem was between the people in the human system. In an effort to solve this problem, I first learned project management and then Agile, which solved a lot of the human system problems inherent to software development.

With Agile, my clients were doing a better job of delivering software, but the IT people were frustrated because of organizational limitations beyond the team's boundaries. They were working in a new way, but they had to wrap it up to look like the old way. It seemed that the senior executives 'didn't get it.' In fact, the executives didn't get it because all they heard about were people collaborating and being empowered, but they couldn't see it reflected in their company's financials. Agile teams were frustrated because they were working hard, but the company seemed to be working against them. One manager said to me, "My bonus rests on this project. It's a key part of the company's strategy, and I have the budget for it. But I can't get anyone to work on it because of the hiring freeze for both contractors and employees."

The problems were beyond the team. It was time to zoom out and look at the overall organization as a system.

"A bad system beats a good person every time."
- W. Edwards Deming

Organizations would traditionally design themselves modeling factories from the industrial revolution. With trains, automobiles, machines, coal, high-volume output was king. Demand was high; the more you could produce, the more you could sell. The industrial revolution was a time when companies valued stability and efficiency over adaptability.

Times have changed. Today mass production has become by mass customization. The barriers to entry for large-scale manufacturing are lower, and it's now possible to do sophisticated manufacturing on a 3D printer in your garage. The differentiator for companies is now their ability to adapt.

Adaptive organizations need new capabilities, different from those developed since the industrial age. Some of the capabilities we develop in individuals also need to be developed at an organizational level. For example, adaptive organizations need the collective capability of emotional intelligence. This is more than a collection of emotionally intelligent individuals; it's operationalized emotional intelligence. Adaptability also means operationalizing resiliency and working through conflict.

Transformational Leaders have a lens to view the organizational capabilities and see what is needed. We'll look at honing this lens and building the skills you need to create new organizational capabilities.

Emergence and Thriving Living Systems

Organizations become adaptive and responsive when we treat them as living systems instead of machines. What does it mean to treat our organization as a living system?

Thriving Living systems have three essential properties[30]:

- *Self-organization* fuels innovation, accountability, collaboration, and productivity
- *Resilience* enables us to thrive in the midst of change and disruption
- *Natural hierarchy* promotes the vitality of the whole by balancing structure and flow, freedom and responsibility, autonomy and coordination, stability, and change

Self-Organization happens when a living system creates a higher order through simple, local actions. An intelligence emerges that is not inherent in any of the parts that make up the whole. Self-organization has been a popular term in organizations for many years, especially in teams, but it is rare to see at the organizational level.

Margaret Wheatley refers to self-organization as "*order for free*." Order emerges from complex systems if you let it. Apply a few simple, local rules and see what emerges. Putting energy into managing thousands of connections is a fool's errand. There's an illusion of control, but even the attempts at control are part of the system. If self-organization gives us "order for free," "we don't need to spend energy creating order. Where should we spend our energy instead? Using a garden analogy, we don't order the plants to grow and tell flowers what color to bloom. However, we make sure the soil is fertile, they have access to sunlight, weeds aren't stealing their nutrients, and animals don't feast on their leaves. We're nurturing our garden and watching it blossom. The delight in a garden is seeing plants

---

30 Donella Meadows as articulated by Sally Parker, TimeZero Enterprises. https://timezeroenterprises.com

bloom in ways we didn't anticipate, letting our nurturing surprise us. The same can happen in an organization.

> *"Don't tell people how to do things; tell them what to do and let them surprise you with their results."*
>
> *- George S. Patton*

When we look at the power in organizations such as social justice movements, we see examples of order for free. A movement happens when people identify with a common cause and do whatever they think will contribute to the cause. There are usually a few simple rules like "save the parks using non-violent means." No one is managing each protest, each task. Every action is different, and there's no concern for consistency. Activists may have access to resources to help them with their cause, but there's no one checking their protest signs for quality, no one rating their performance. If it works, they do it again; if it doesn't, they don't. They find each other and collaborate on what's working, and they combine efforts to amplify their message. What are the leaders doing? Social justice leaders provide resources to the activists; they speak publicly to clarify and consolidate the message. They don't manage the activists or coordinate activities. They cultivate and nurture the movement.

Resilience in an organization means that the organization is both flexible and strong enough to withstand change. In a living organization, this also means that the system creates its own resiliency. Resiliency is a capability that comes from inside the organization; it's not something that you can from a vendor. The thing that does come from outside the organization is information. The organization uses information from outside to learn and grow its resiliency.

In 2020, the COVID-19 crisis uncovered a weakness: hospitals couldn't quickly increase supplies and capacity for a spike in patients. Many blamed the weakness on years of "just in time inventory," which reduced supplies to almost nothing because there was no supply they couldn't get within hours. There was also a push for outpatient procedures, reducing the number of beds in a facility. When COVID-19 hit, hospitals were ill-equipped to handle the increased volume. There was a push for hospitals to stockpile supplies and add capacity. But resilience emerged through makeshift hospitals, home-sewn masks, and other self-organizing activities. Instead of stockpiling, could hospitals have been more resilient leading into the crisis? Perhaps more transparency into supply-chain and contingency plans for increasing patient capacity. This example calls out a common tension between fortification and resilience.

It also highlights the tension between internal and external as it applies to resiliency. The hospital's internal resiliency showed when they built makeshift units, masks and looked to find supply chain solutions. They use external information from vendors on supply chain visibility and government support to inform their own resiliency.

Natural Hierarchy means that we enable flow through hierarchies that are naturally in service to each other. Hierarchy is the organization of systems and subsystems. As recurring "branching" patterns that we see everywhere, hierarchies arise naturally to enhance the flow of the 'current' (i.e., materials, information, nutrients, resources …) flowing through a system. In natural systems, hierarchies work with friction to find new ways to improve flow.

The word "hierarchy" has become villainized because it has a connotation with "power over" and "superiority." "If you look at living systems, there are natural hierarchies everywhere, but without the human concept of "superiority." A tree, for example, has hierarchy in the trunk, branches, leaves, and buds. But the trunk is not the boss. The leaves are in service to bringing food to the roots via sunlight, and the roots are in service to the leaves by sending nutrients.

There are organizational frameworks that claim to eliminate hierarchy, but they do have a hierarchy if you look closely. What they attempt to remove is "superiority." In a living organization, no one feels inferior because the hierarchy levels do not have power over lower levels; they all serve each other. Hierarchy balances the welfare, freedoms, and responsibilities of the subsystems and total system, ensuring enough central control to achieve coordination toward the large-system goal and enough autonomy to keep all subsystems flourishing, functioning, and self-organizing. It provides both stability and adaptability and reduces the amount of information that any part of the system keeps track of. The difference is in scope, some teams are deep and narrow, and others are broad and shallow.

When we view organizations through the lens of living systems, instead of treating them like machines, we create expansiveness and new possibilities for what the organization can become.

Journal Exercise: Identify places or practices in your organization where the emergence of the living system is hampered, perhaps by mechanistic thinking. How might you introduce living systems properties to these areas?

Organizational Tensions

A *tension* is two seemingly opposing forces that are interdependent[31]. When well-managed, organizational tensions can create breakthroughs. When managed poorly, they can be devastating. Questions like, "Do you want high quality or low cost?" "Do you want stability or innovation?" are the false dichotomies that plague us in corporate life. They seem to be paradoxes, where you can't have both. If we take a closer look, we find that they are tensions between two complementary ends. When wielded creatively, these tensions can produce new possibilities. When wielded as a choice, one or the other, these tensions do the exact opposite, creativity shuts down, and the system flounders.

All living systems naturally have a set of tensions, also known as polarities[32]. Managing tensions well can be generative - generating health and life. Poorly managed tensions can create dysfunction or death.

A *tension* is two seemingly opposing forces that are interdependent and structurally connected to a greater goal. Let's break that down. How can two opposing forces be interdependent? A simple example is breathing. You need to both inhale and exhale to live. They are opposites, interdependent, and both connect to the structure of the lungs and oxygen delivery system. If you choose only one, either exhale or inhale, you'll die.

To clarify a common misunderstanding, "AND thinking" does not mean that we're going to do everything all the time. I have seen companies proclaim that they are an "AND Company" and

31 Based on the work by Barry Johnson, Polarity Partnerships.

32 Sally Parker, TimeZero Enterprises, https://timezeroenterprises.com

proceed to dilute their impact while working their people to death. 'AND' does not mean we compromise on everything; it means we get creative about considering both. When we say "AND thinking," we actually mean "AND/OR," we consider both. Sometimes it's an OR. For example, when we say, "stability and change," this does not mean being half as stable and half as changing. And it doesn't mean just working twice as much so we can do both. It means taking a very close look at how we can use change in service to stability and use our stability to spark change. Can we loosen stability in specific places to open innovation? Instead of putting the risk officer in the arena with the innovation officer and having them battle it out to the death, they create shared goals and collaborate on how to meet them.

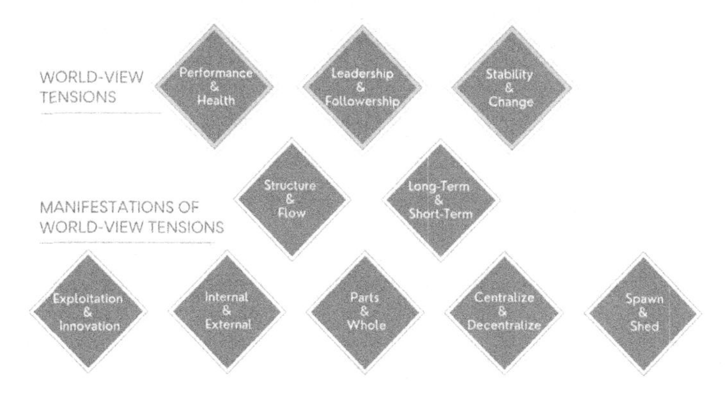

Performance and Health is a tension between the force that gets an organization where it needs to go and the force that keeps the organization in good working order. Visualize this tension as a car's GPS versus the dashboard. The GPS guides the car along the most efficient route, while the dashboard helps keep the vehicle operational. A driver that only looks at their dashboard has an excellent understanding of the car's condition but has no idea where they're going, and vice versa.

Leadership and Followership is a tension between pointing the direction and creating supportive conditions and active movement in that direction. This tension is not about formal roles but what the organization needs in the moment to thrive. An individual can be both a leader and a follower, and neither can succeed without the other.

Stability and change describe the tension between how organizations need stability to operate while also being ready to change and adapt when necessary. Current trends are causing conflict in this tension, where those advocating for stability are separate and pitted against those pushing for change. A generative tension[33] energizes people with shared purpose and helps them work on creative ways to embrace change while protecting stability.
Structure and Flow is tension between creating just enough structure that enhances the flow without impeding it. When these tensions work together, the structure not only enables flow, but is also continuously informed and shaped by the flow.

Long-Term and Short-Term thinking are often seen as either/or, but when we look at different time horizons 'in service to each other,' decisions become clearer. An example is when a short-term solution will require long-term rework. The long-term side refuses anything requiring rework, while the short-term insists on a quick fix. Can they serve each other by having the quick fix generate revenue to fund the long-term goals without undermining them? Looking at the interplay between the time horizons can open new possibilities.

Exploitation and Innovation uses the term *exploitation* in a positive sense, meaning leveraging current assets. An example of this is the sales team that sells the cash cow product

33 Sally Parker, TimeZero Enterprises. https://timezeroenterprises.com

instead of new products (or vice versa). A traditional approach incentivizes sales reps to push the latest products, leaving them an unbalanced economic choice, which detracts from products with proven reliability and appeal. A generative tension might link the products together, helping them sell each other.

Internal and External tensions exist between methods of information gathering. Some organizations gather information mainly from internal sources, such as employees, while others focus on external sources: customers, vendors, and competitors. There is a danger in becoming too internally facing, but a similar risk exists in being too reactive to external sources. An organization can unmoor itself from its internal identity, shaping its actions purely through customer whims.

Parts and Whole reflects the tension between the needs of the whole and the needs of the parts. The industrial revolution and Newtonian science created an over-focus on reductionist thinking: the process of breaking things down into their component parts to find and fix a problem. In mechanistic systems, this often works. But in living, complex systems, reductionist thinking has unintended consequences. Fixing something in one area breaks something else, as the whole has a different or more complex set of behaviors than its parts. Lean Thinking calls this 'local optimization' and 'global optimization'; what's good for the part may not be good for the whole and vice versa. Individuals and teams need to be cared for and considered, while also considering and caring for the whole organization.

Centralize and Decentralize is the ongoing tension between concentrated and distributed structures. As organizations grow larger, economies of scale often drive them to become more centralized to improve efficiency. An unintended consequence of this is the creation of collective intelligence that struggles with innovative thinking and local relevance. Today, many organizations are looking to decentralize their intelligence. An example of this is the shift from functional organizations to cross-functional teams. Generative tension looks to leverage the upside of both centralization and decentralization.

Spawn and Shed is the tension that exists between spawning new and shedding that which is obsolete. Finding an organization that can balance both these tasks is rare, and it's more common to see these activities take place in response to a crisis or one-off event. Generative tensions spark continuous reflection on what needs to be born and what needs to die inside an organization.

Organizational Transformations tend to oscillate or "lurch" between ends of the tension. This oscillation is the organizational equivalent of gasping for air. Consider the example of an organization that has focused on stability for 100 years. A new CEO comes in, looks around, and proclaims, "this organization needs to change or die!" Hundreds of initiatives crop up, focusing the company's resources on innovation and change. Then one day, a crisis happens. Because of the lack of focus on stability, the company loses a big customer, gets some bad press, or the stock price drops. The company becomes aware that it lost focus on stability, and a mandate comes down to shift the focus back to stability. The pendulum swings, but the company hasn't advanced.

Journal Exercise: What tensions are most present in your organization? What is the greater purpose of each opposing force? What is the deeper fear underneath each? How can the tension become more generative and less destructive? Try having this discussion with people who have opposing viewpoints.

Adaptive Challenges

"The single biggest failure of leadership is to treat Adaptive Challenges like Technical Problems."
- Ronald A. Heifetz & Marty Linky

Transformational leaders solve Adaptive Challenges, but when they mistakenly treat them like a Technical Problem, they fail. Key skills for a Transformational Leader are: knowing the difference between Technical Problems and Adaptive Challenges, being able to overcome an organization's attachment to Technical Problems, and then finally, working through Adaptive Challenges.

What is the difference between a Technical Problem and an Adaptive Challenge?

A *Technical Problem* is a problem that has an answer or a few possible answers. These challenges are bounded, meaning that the answer lies within the boundary of the problem. The answers to Technical Problems can be solved with the help of an expert and implemented through processes or tools. Machines are full of Technical Problems. Technical Problems are relatively easy to understand; they are linear, the cause and effect are testable. For this reason, people are generally receptive to answers for Technical Problems.

In a complexity model, such as Cynefin[34], Technical Problems are generally simple or complicated but not complex or chaotic. We solve Technical Problems through deductive reasoning; the continuous elimination of variables exposes the problem.

34 https://en.wikipedia.org/wiki/Cynefin_framework

If you have a broken radio, that's a technical problem. The answer is within the boundary of the radio. An expert can fix it, and you probably need a screwdriver and a new resistor (tools). A Technical Problem doesn't have to involve technology. Like a radio, it could be much simpler, like "What do I do when I pull a muscle?" where the possible answers are "stretch, ice, heat, movement." The answer is bounded within the body, so I might seek the advice of a physical therapist or an orthopedist.

An *Adaptive Challenge* is a case where there is no clear answer or set of answers. The challenges are unbounded, as external forces impact the challenge. The intelligence in an Adaptive system often lies within the connections, not the 'nodes,' making it difficult to see. Living systems are full of Adaptive Challenges. These challenges are 'Complex Systems,' those where a change doesn't yield a predictable outcome. This lack of predictability explains why when you use a Technical Problem approach to an Adaptive Challenge; you end up with something hearkening back to the song, "There was an Old Lady Who Swallowed a Fly." Each solution yields new and unforeseen problems. Adaptive Challenges are not solved so much as they are continually taking shape. The complexity and unpredictability of Adaptive Challenges are difficult to grasp, so people attempt to convert them into Technical Problems.

If you think of an invasive species decimating an ecosystem, this is an Adaptive Challenge. As humans try to correct the invasive species, they often find that they only make it worse. There's a commonly cited story about Macquarie Island, off the coast of Australia, where the attempt to eradicate an invasive species of mice and rats continued to enlarge the problem. Here you start to see something reminiscent of "There was an Old Lady Who Swallowed a Fly." Rats and mice first arrived in the 1800s on the ships of seal hunters. The government tried to control the rat population by adding cats. But then feral cats were overrunning the island and killing the seabirds. Humans decided to eradicate the cats with a virus. As it turns out, rabbits are immune to the virus, and without the cats, the rabbit population has multiplied like...rabbits. And so, it goes.

When we think about the organizations we work in, the challenges we face are usually Adaptive. The good news is, having Adaptive Challenges means that we have the potential to adapt! The not-so-good news is that Adaptive Challenges are fundamentally more difficult for groups to accept and incorporate.

"In the face of adaptive pressures, people don't want questions; they want answers"

- Ronald A. Heifetz & Marty Linky, Leadership on the Line

When pressure mounts, people are looking for answers, pain relief, a way out. That's why silver bullet solutions are so popular. Leaders may think, "even if the solution causes a problem elsewhere, at least it's not in my shop." Our role as Transformational Leaders is to help people understand that they are solving Adaptive Challenges. Heifetz and Linky articulate this clearly in the following quote:

> *"In mobilizing adaptive work, you have to engage people in adjusting their unrealistic expectations, rather than try to satisfy them as if the situation were amenable to a technical remedy. You have to counteract their exaggerated dependency and promote their resourcefulness. This takes an extraordinary level of presence, time and artful communication, but it may also take more time and trust than you have."*
>
> - Ronald A. Heifetz & Marty Linky,
> *Leadership on the Line*

Being aware of the type of challenge you are facing will help move you into the right approach. With Adaptive Challenges, you'll need to take a broad look at the whole system and how activities and strategies impact and affect each other.

Journal Exercise: How are you or your organization viewing transformation as a Technical Problem? What would need to happen to shift into thinking of it as an Adaptive Challenge?

Systems Thinking – Interconnectedness

Did you ever wonder why so many business fads have so much trouble getting traction? Often, it's because they solve a part of the problem, but they don't consider the whole system. Systems have intelligence and behavior that do not exist in any one of their elements. It's impossible to solve the challenges of the whole by examining the parts.

> *"A system consists of three kinds of things: elements, interconnections, and a function or purpose."*[35]
>
> *- Donella Meadows*

Systems Thinking means that we consider the whole system, how it works together, beyond each part. We look not only at the whole, right now; we also look at it over time. We might ask questions like, "Who else is impacted by this problem? Who might be affected by the change? How might a change unfold in the future?

Systems Thinking is a paradigm shift from "Reductionism" popularized by Fredrick Winslow Taylor in the early 1900s. Reductionism rests on the idea that if you *reduce* the system

35 Meadows, Donella H.. Thinking in Systems (p. 11). Chelsea Green Publishing. Kindle Edition.

down to its component parts, then optimize each part, you will optimize the system. Reductionism works well for Technical Problems, and it resonated so much with how our brains work that it has stuck around for over 100 years. Unfortunately, it doesn't work for complex, adaptive systems. My chiropractor likens this to building each muscle in the body without teaching the muscles to work together. She said this integration is essential to prevent injury because the problem isn't solely the muscle; it's the connection between the muscles. When you reduce a system to its parts, you lose the information contained in the connections.

System behavior is emergent; it transcends its own boundaries. This phenomenon is evident when we look at the growth of cities. The Dallas "Metroplex" has expanded past the boundaries of Dallas to include everything in between the neighboring city of Fort Worth. The Dallas Metroplex largely results from an urban system left to run wild, resulting in traffic, pollution, and urban decay. In contrast, cities like Portland, Oregon, have attempted "Smart Growth" that includes policies like boundaries on the urban area, public transportation, bike lanes, and preserved green spaces. As with all complex, adaptive systems, some of the efforts yielded unpredictable results. Still, overall, Portland has created a much healthier, more productive city than those in urban sprawl. Smart Growth cities are a great example of creating conditions for a healthy system without trying to control it.

Transformations are complex systems. Transformations fail when we treat them as parts and put artificial boundaries on them. Look at your transformation efforts as a whole system, and find ways to cultivate it rather than control it.

Journal Exercise: Where is your transformation under bounded or over bounded? Are there areas where the transformation efforts have been approached as "parts" without viewing the "whole"?

Correlation is not Causation (aka stop seeking Best Practices and Benchmarks)

Living Systems are complex, adaptive systems; complex adaptive systems are systems in which the same inputs don't always yield the same result. In business, we like everything to be linear; I press a button, and out pops a widget. Living systems don't work that way.

It's important to realize that we cannot reverse-engineer complex, adaptive systems. I can take apart a radio, figure out how it works, and make my own radio. (or at least I like to think I can). The output of a complex, adaptive system will not lead you to the inputs because the whole is different than the parts. I bet you thought I was going to say, "the whole is greater than the parts," but I didn't; I said "different." The system has intelligence that doesn't live in any of its parts, so you can't dissect it to see how it works.

Companies that copy the output of successful companies don't achieve the same success as those they copy. They mistakenly correlate the outcome with the cause. For example, successful Silicon Valley companies are known for having ping pong tables so employees can blow off steam. When older, legacy companies installed ping pong tables, no one used them, and even when they did, it had no impact on productivity. Why? The ping pong tables were a correlation, not causation. Because people worked hard and companies were successful, they needed some way to blow off steam, so they got some ping pong tables. Ping pong tables did not cause success; the ping pong tables were simply correlated to success.

Using *"best practices"* is another way companies copy the result instead of the cause. Everyone who has ever worked with me knows that I cringe at the term *"best practices."* "Best practice" suggests that there's one way, one best way, and if we do that, then we'll be golden. In a complex, adaptive system, this is never true. Proven, repeatable activities such as "doctors must wash their hands" or "cooks must use gloves when handling food" absolutely call for best practices. But when we are talking about transforming large, complex, human systems with infinite variables and unique identities, there is very little that we can boil down to a single best practice.

I was working with a client who led an organization steeped in authority and control. The leaders went on a site visit to Google to find out how to be more like Google. They came back with one key finding, "Google only allows programmers to choose from four programming languages." I said, "is that all you saw on your visit?" They truly believed this was the key to what they had been doing wrong. The fact is that Google is not an organization based on authority and control; Google runs on a more open organizational model, where people are empowered, participatory and exploratory. Presumably, Google found that perhaps the boundaries were too loose, a proliferation of programming languages started to cause compatibility and maintainability issues, so they collaboratively narrowed it down to four. The same constraint caused a very different result in a company like Google that recognized it needed a little more structure than it would in a company already choking under bureaucracy. My client mistook the correlation, limiting programming languages, for the cause of efficient software development.

"Industry benchmarks" are another area where companies correlate their output with competitors instead of looking for causes. I ask clients what they will do with the industry benchmark. What decisions will you make based on that information? They answer that they want to make sure they are in line with their industry, or maybe a little better, and decide there's nothing to do. Or perhaps they are worse than their industry in a particular area, so they need to improve. In the words of countless parents everywhere, "If they all jump off the Empire State Building, will you jump too?" Industry benchmarks are all about ranking and give no information that is valuable for the future. The decision criteria for changing spending in a particular area, or implementing a new process, should not be because your competitors are doing it. It's exactly the opposite; you want to do it because your competitors are NOT doing it. A client asked me, "What are the industry benchmarks on innovation? We don't want to be innovative unless we know what it will yield." What?! That is wrong on so many levels. You don't want to innovate until you know your competitors are innovating? And you want to discover something unknown only when we know what it is? Industry benchmarks show some correlation to your competitors and success, but benchmark measures have no bearing on what causes an organization to be successful. Continuing the words of parents everywhere, "you worry about you."

What does all this mean for us as Transformational Leaders? It means that copying another organization's best practices won't give you the same result they got. Looking at benchmarks won't help you. What works for others may not work for you. Is there anything valuable to learn from others? Yes, please go learn and experiment with other people's practices! See what works for your organization. In terms of benchmarks, look outside your industry. What can you, a shipping company, learn from video gaming? What can a bank learn from a clothing designer? Look in unusual places for inspiration.

Journal Exercise: What transformation practices have you, or your organization, chosen because they were correlated with success? How might you position those practices as experiments? If benchmarking is used in your organization, consider whether it is an effective use of energy. Where else might that energy be directed?

Organizational Emotional Intelligence

We know we need to build emotional intelligence as individuals, but what does that mean as an organizational capability? Is there a difference between a collection of emotionally intelligent individuals and an emotionally intelligent organization? And if there is a difference, how do you build an emotionally intelligent organization?

Let's think of the emotional intelligence of individuals as "nodes" and the emotional intelligence between individuals as the connections between nodes. Organizational emotional intelligence is the environment and conditions where those nodes exist. Building intelligence in those connections is something we do naturally as humans. But we're blocked by all the "stuff," our own emotions, policy, process, etc. Our job as Leaders is less about 'building' and 'directing' organizational emotional intelligence and more about creating conditions for it to happen.

> *"When we push individuals for EQ, it allows organizations to bypass systemic issues. Individuals end up shouldering the organizational shame, and it's not enough to get the*

organization out of the shame box."
- paraphrased from Sonya Renee Taylor

What does an Emotionally Intelligent Organization look and feel like? Emotional intelligence at the organizational level starts with a clear identity. We build on identity by applying the same characteristics we applied to the individual, "The Me." Self-awareness, emotional literacy, courage, curiosity, resiliency, and recovery.

Organizational Identity. The identity of an organization defines who we are. What are we good at? What are our values? According to Margaret Wheatly, "Identity is the sense-making capacity of the organization."[36] If an organization lacks a cohesive identity, the structure just becomes a set of rules. A shared identity sets the stage for the organization to adapt. Again, from Margaret Wheatly, "People use their shared sense of identity to organize their unique contributions." You will not foresee the many ways the organization needs to adapt; it's imperative that the organization intake information, make sense of it and apply it in ways that are not yet known. Identity provides decision criteria for which opportunities to pursue and which to ignore.

Many companies have started organizing themselves in a customer-centric model. And while customers are vital for the livelihood of any business, too many companies let the customer define their identity. When this happens, the company can become like a squirrel, chasing one customer's impulse to the next. When the company is grounded in its identity, it is less likely to react to customer whims.

---

36 Margaret Wheatly, The Irresistible Future of Organizing, 1996.

A strong, clear organizational identity is the anchor for Emotional Intelligence as an Organization. To show Emotional Intelligence, the organization needs a cohesive understanding of who they are; otherwise, it's easy to become fractured and reactive.

The Self-Aware Organization. In the first section of this book, we defined the dimensions of self-awareness for an individual as 1) awareness of one's own emotions and 2) awareness of one's impact on others. Similarly, at the organizational level, the organization as a whole is reflecting on its own identity, how it feels, and its impact.

Consider the tension between stability and change that arises between two divisions, perhaps it's finance and product development. Finance doesn't want to invest in new products that can't guarantee a high return, and product development knows they can't have a winning product without experimentation. Often this ends with a compromise that placates both groups, such as "we'll invest only in products that can prove some threshold of revenue in the first year."

Consider a different scenario where the two groups are at odds, but they put the company at the center—the discussion shifts to what the "company wants" and how each group can meet that desire. Finance and product development still have their perspectives, but the discussion centers on the company's needs, not the needs of the divisions. Using our example, if the company wants to be leading-edge with innovative products, finance might devise a way to manage product investment before they have a projected return. Another company might want to double down on opportunities from existing assets, in which case product development might focus on innovation that builds revenue from existing products. The discussion shifts away from the opposition between the groups and moves into collaboration in service to the organization.

When we take it up even one level higher, we might consider how our decision affects the company's impact, both internally and externally. In terms of "impact on others," I hear many organizations talk about the impact on customers, shareholders, and sometimes even employees, but rarely do I hear a discussion on the impact to society at large or the environment. Those are traditionally viewed as "risk management" activities, and rather than being brought into the center, they are managed off to the side. The decisions are implicit, and no one has a chance to discuss the impact. When we shift the company's impact into the center, we make space to address and acknowledge the impact explicitly.

Asking ourselves, "how is the company feeling and what is its impact?" creates self-awareness for the organization as a whole. You will be surprised at what emerges.

The Emotionally Literate Organization. Does your organization know how it feels? You know that there's a feeling to a place or a company even if you're working remotely. We can sense the sentiment of a group or even a company. Even different departments have their own emotions. In the early 90s, I started my first corporate job for a behemoth telecom company. When I told people in other parts of the company that I worked in IT, they always seemed to scowl at me and roll their eyes, and sometimes it was even followed by insults like "that whole department should be fired." I quickly learned that IT was the most hated department in the company. I noticed that my co-workers would save themselves the embarrassment by introducing themselves without saying the department's name; they would instead say which business unit they supported.

Inside the organization, we were like bullied kids, trying desperately to get on the bully's good side while also laying low so as not to draw attention to ourselves. Between IT and the other departments, there was a lot of blame, finger-pointing, and a ton of processes in an attempt to resolve conflict through rules. But what I rarely saw was an acknowledgment of the emotions between the groups.

An emotionally literate organization is aware of its emotional impact on others and their partner organization's emotional impact on them. These emotions are named and addressed. Like with individuals, by naming and addressing organizational emotions, we can start healing them and then change them.

The Deeply Curious Organization. When an organization is deeply curious, they make space for exploration. FedEx and Google are famous for giving people 10% of their time for ideation. If you've ever asked a question in a meeting and gotten shut down for it being off-topic or irrelevant, you know what the opposite of a curious organization looks like. This dismissal of questions doesn't happen just because one person is a jerk; it is allowed because the organization values execution more than exploration. When organizations value execution over exploration, they define value as a threshold that they can't fall below, giving up the opportunity to far surpass the goal. In an organization like this, there's absolutely no reason for people to risk meeting the goal for a chance to exceed it. One condition that cultivates a curious organization is by relaxing narrow goals and dates. Inflexible deadlines and goals discourage exploration, even when it could improve the timeline and goal. Another condition for creating a curious organization is to model appreciation for curiosity and exploration, whether or not it manifests in value. That last part is essential. Valuing exploration and curiosity even if it doesn't pan out.

I worked with an organization that needed new products to replace their declining ones, so they established an innovation team. Their team's mandate was that a) they had to use an innovation model that was proven to work, and b) innovative ideas would only receive funding if they were guaranteed to make at least $50M in the first three years. They were asking for innovation without allowing for exploration. Curiosity was missing; they were looking to check an innovation box. I'll let you guess how that turned out.

The Courageous Organization. With individuals, what looks like courage to others, feels like weakness inside us. With organizations, it works in the exact reverse; when an organization has courage, on the outside, it can look to us like risk and weakness. In 2007, when Apple decided to build the iPhone, they had no prior experience in telecom. A few big players dominated the wireless telecom device market, and Apple was not one of them. And to launch a phone, Apple would need to be available on a network controlled by even fewer, very large companies. Despite the barriers to entry, Apple dumped a lot of money into developing the device. And despite being a new and small entrant into the market, Apple wanted a higher share of revenue than any of the existing device manufacturers. One of the large network providers practically laughed in Steve Jobs' face. Who did this guy think he was? The network provider refused to carry the iPhone, which turned out to be a bad move as the iPhone quickly began to dominate the market.

With the iPhone, inside Apple, it looks like they are following their heart, stepping into something in which they truly believed. On the outside, it looked like they were not living in reality, making foolish investments and demands. Organizational courage comes from the collective, knowing their identity, and staying grounded in it. Conversations raise questions like "what should we do, based on who we are?" rather than simply "how can we make money?" The organization is listening to its inner voice.

The Resilient Organization. Like individuals, organizations can condition themselves for resiliency by knowing their identity, self-worth, and values.

Clarity on an organization's values helps it stay resilient because it's not sinking energy in conflicting values. In the face of disruption, an organization without clear, shared values will get into an endless debate on how to respond. By trying to satisfy a broad set of values, solutions can become both rigid and watered down. For example, if a competitor launches a product that threatens your company's market share, some may argue that a quick response is critical, while others want to ensure that the response is high quality, even if slower. Which do you choose? There is no right answer; it depends on the company's values. Does the company value a high-quality customer experience with a loyal following or value being on the bleeding edge of innovation, first to market, attracting early adopters? If you're not clear on this, the same arguments will come up for thousands of activities and tasks.

Organizational Recovery. Organizational recovery is the same as individual recovery in that it starts with allowing itself to sit with a feeling and reflect on what's behind the collective emotion. For example, think about an organization that launches a product that's a complete failure in the market. Traditional organizations ask, "How did this happen? Who is responsible? How do we make sure it never happens again?" Transformational Organizations shift the focus to how they can bounce back quickly. They know it will happen again; if not the same failure, they will have other failures. I hear leaders say, "we allow failure, but not the same way twice." Fair enough, but you just failed in one way, and there are infinite ways to fail in the future. Where do you want to put your energy? Fortifying against that one way of failing or recovering from the endless ways you're going to fail in the future? Transformational leaders operationalize recovery capabilities so that they have room for failure.

How do we create conditions for recovery? We build structures to handle failure when it happens instead of building structures that prevent failure from occurring. When new teams do their initial chartering, I'll ask them, "How do you want to be with each other when you fail?" Organizations should ask themselves the same question. When we fail, how will we behave? Will we find out who is to blame and make some heads roll? Or will we let the team who failed determine what's next? Do we have a policy of punishing failure or nurturing and learning from failure? I know it's popular today to say how much we all celebrate failure, but I haven't seen too many organizations reflect this in people's performance reviews. When an organization knows it can recover, it expands the risks it can take within wider bounds of recovery.

Conclusion. Organizations can build Emotional Intelligence. An organization becomes soulful by attending to its identity, self-awareness, emotional literacy, courage, curiosity, resiliency, and recovery.

Journal Exercise: What is the identity of your organization? Take a random sample of other people in your organization and see if you get a consistent answer. How does your organization fare in the areas of self-awareness, emotional literacy, courage, curiosity, resiliency, and recovery? How can you help your organization work on its emotional intelligence?

The Soulful Organization

What does it mean for an organization to have soul? Perhaps it's easier to start by looking at the reverse; what does it look like when an organization lacks soul? Internally, soulless organizations have palpable toxicity, strained relationships, and people are out for individual survival. Externally, a soulless organization looks like a company that lacks purpose and identity. When a company says one thing, but its actions are contradictory, we sense that the company doesn't have soul. When a company hurts its employees, preys on its customers, and damages the community, it is not a soulful company. A soulful company is clear on who they are and lives by their values. When a company has soul, there's an ethos that draws internal and external people into wanting to sustain it. A Transformational Leader is the custodian of the soul of an organization.

Organizations are living systems, and soul fuels living systems. A Transformational Leader's job is to breathe new life into an organization, and therefore a Transformational Leader must attend to the organization's soul. The **5 Steps to Soul in the Workplace**[37] framework is a simple tool to start doing this. The changes will be subtle at first, but you'll see them grow over time.

The 5 Steps to Soul in the Workplace is a framework to work through alone or with a team. You can apply this process to micro or macro situations in your workplace. I recommend starting with something small, maybe staff meetings, and working your way up to something like budget planning.

37 SoulsAtWork.org

The 5 steps are:

1. **What is the soulful purpose?**
2. **What makes it soul-crushing?**
3. **Where does it violate Power, Freedom, and Connection?**
4. **What tensions are at play?**
5. **What would it take to bring in soul?**

1. What is the soulful purpose? Ask, "Why do we have this soulless process in the first place"? Put all cynicism aside for a moment, save that for step 2. What is the real reason we need this process, or why did someone think we needed it?

You may have to dig deep; try asking the "5 whys" to get to the heart of the process. The purpose will be important later when we re-imagine the process; purpose will be part of our design criteria.

2. What makes it soul-crushing? Now here's where we get to vent. If there's a lot of pent-up frustration, you might even start with this step. Let it out; what do you hate about this process? If you're working in a team, you might facilitate this as anonymous brainstorming.

You've got to 'name it to tame it!'[38] You want to know all the things that are crushing people's souls so that you can re-imagine a process without the soul-crushing parts.

3. Where does it violate Power, Freedom, and Connection? Once we have all vented, we'll try to unpack those complaints into violations of the three tenets of soul; Power, Freedom, and Connection.

38 Mark Brackett, Permission to Feel.

Power is violated when we can't take the actions we need to be effective and fulfilled in our work. It doesn't feel good when someone has power over us, especially when it prevents us from exercising our power.

Freedom is violated when fear causes us to go against our values. We see this when we agree to bad decisions so we won't lose our bonus or protect our job.

Connection is violated when we break the trust and human connection with others. This can happen in many ways, like when we feel the company has mistreated a customer, when we're pitted against our peers or when we have to lay people off.

Apply each of these three tenets, Power, Freedom, and Connection, to your situation to get clear on which ones are violated and why.

4. What tensions are at play? Tensions are as seemingly opposing forces that we can leverage together for generative purposes. In other words, what opposing forces are pulling us apart, that could be pulling us together? At this point, just answer the first part, what forces are pulling us apart? Reference the Organizational Tension chapter for ideas on what tension(s) might be at play.

5. What would it take to bring in soul? At this point, you've unpacked the baggage that was sucking the soul from your process. Take a moment to breathe, take a break, and when you reconvene, ask the question, "what would it take to bring in soul?" If you could create a dream budget planning process, how would it look? Steps 1-4 give you your design criteria; step 5 asks you to use your imagination. Design thinking tools can help with this step.

Applying the **5 Steps to Soul in the Workplace** in your organization shifts how people view the organization. It gives them permission and paves the way to re-imagine a more soulful organization.

Journal Exercise: Choose a process or practice in your organization that seems to lack soul-Journal through the **5 Steps to Soul in the Workplace** with the soulless process or practice in mind. Try working through the 5 steps with a group of people.

Power Dynamics and Politics

Transformational leadership is a political role. I have seen many people take on this role and say, "I like the job except the politics." With full love and respect, I'll tell you what I tell them "The whole job is politics; if you don't like politics, this is not a good fit for you."

How do you react when you hear the word "Politics"? How about "Power"?

When I ask organizations about the political landscape, people get their backs up immediately. They'll tell me, "We don't have politics here!" And often, I hear this from the biggest politicians in the organization. When people deny the existence of politics, they're saying that either they don't want to acknowledge it or don't want to upset the existing politics. Remember when we talked about current reality and future state? Politics is one of those things that are important in the current reality and might be less important in your future state. But you're not going to get the future state if you can't navigate the current reality.
We can't effectively dance with Power and Politics until we reckon with our relationship with these words. Let's start with

politics. Do you feel yourself bristle when you read that word?

Politics is the practice of actively navigating the human system. Since organizations are human systems, to lead transformations, you'll have to be able to navigate them. Some people like to soften the word by saying 'change agent' or 'organizational dynamics,' but I don't feel these words truly capture the finesse and savvy that's called for. I haven't yet found another word that captures the meaning and the punchiness of 'politics.'

In a pure mechanistic system, you would not have politics. For years we have approached organizations as machines, acting like politics were a pest. Politics keeps cropping up in mechanistic organizations because organizations are not, in fact, machines.

Power in an organization is the flow of influence and priority in the organization. Power ties back to our discussion on energy; power comes from energy. Common sources of power are authority, economics, or personality. Economics means that if your department brings in a lot of money, you typically have a lot of power. Power can be hidden and informal; it doesn't always follow the organizational hierarchy. Think about the gatekeepers, who shape what an executive hears and sees. The gatekeepers often have more power than the executive behind the gate.

In *Political Savvy,* Joel DeLuca, Ph.D.[39] asks these two questions about where you stand on politics:

- Which statement best reflects your actions regarding politics:
    1. I initiate most of the politics that happen in my workplace.

39 Political Savvy by Joel DeLuca, Ph.D.

2. I can read the political tea leaves, but I don't always get involved.
3. I don't get involved in politics; I just respond to the result.

- Which statement best reflects your view of workplace politics:
    - A. Politics are a zero-sum game. There's only one winner.
    - B. Politics are a necessary part of the workplace.
    - C. I believe that politics is an exciting and fun way to get things done.

Based on your answers, Joel DeLuca asks that you place yourself on this grid:

ACTION ORIENTATION	POLITICS VIEWED AS: NEGATIVE	NEUTRAL	POSITIVE
INITIATES	MACHIAVELLIAN • Manipulator • Looks out for #1	RESPONSIBLE • Obligation • Comes with Territory	LEADER • Play Maker • Impact Player
PREDICTS	PROTECTOR • File Builder • Defensive	SPECULATOR • Grapeviner	ADVISOR • Counselor
RESPONDS	CYNIC • I told you so • Gossip	FATALIST • Que Sera Sera	SPECTATOR • Fan • Encourager

As Transformational Leaders, we need to operate in cells C1 or minimally a B1 in this grid. If you are leading a transformation, you've got to be initiating the action; you cannot be reacting to actions undertaken by others. Initiating action ties back to responsibility; you are creating, taking responsibility for making things happen. On the top axis, I hope it goes without saying that we want to view politics in a positive light, creating win-win and abundance. A negative view creates scarcity and views politics as a zero-sum game. Being manipulative and self-centered is not transformational. It's essential to know how to navigate all types, but also know that people are movable.

Don't write someone off as Machiavellian; dig in a bit; they may be a product of their system.

Politics don't have to be dirty. Politics simply means that you are actively navigating the human system of an organization. Whatever you choose to call it, it's the keystone of your success. A Transformational Leader is adept at both politics and power. If you don't have a clear map of the human system, you won't be able to navigate your way through it. Getting yourself aligned with the flow of power is a key skill. Being able to map the political landscape is also a key skill.

Navigating the flow of power requires you to know where the power lives and how it moves. For example, many organizations have a PMO or other governance group that manages 'resource allocation.' This team or individual has tremendous power over what gets worked on and what doesn't, and this power can override and undermine the CEO's strategic direction. In this instance, the governance group has more power than the CEO. The CEO may have hired you for Transformation, but you won't succeed if you can't affect the power coming from governance. In this example, finding ways to channel the power from the governance team will be a critical factor in your success. There are tools and techniques to help you do this. But all tools will require your own strategic thinking in your specific context. In the example above, you might work collaboratively with the governance team, convince the CEO to alter the governance team, or perhaps create some transparency to the impact of the governance decisions. Depending on the situation, the relationships, and the severity of the impact, you'll have to use your judgment.

Political Landscape maps are a beautiful tool for gaining clarity on the human system and dynamics at play. Many great leaders intuitively map the political landscape in their minds. One benefit of a physical map is gathering and seeing information and perspectives from multiple people. If you're working on a transformation team, team members may have different information on the relationships between individuals and groups. These different perspectives add richness to the model. Another great benefit to a physical map is that your team can collaboratively strategize, looking at the same picture. Think about how the strategy sounds without a physical map; people keep throwing in the information they have and argue approaches in the air in a hypothetical, opinion-centric way. When there's a map in the center of the discussion, proposed strategies are visible and overlay a common visual. New strategies emerge from the combined data.

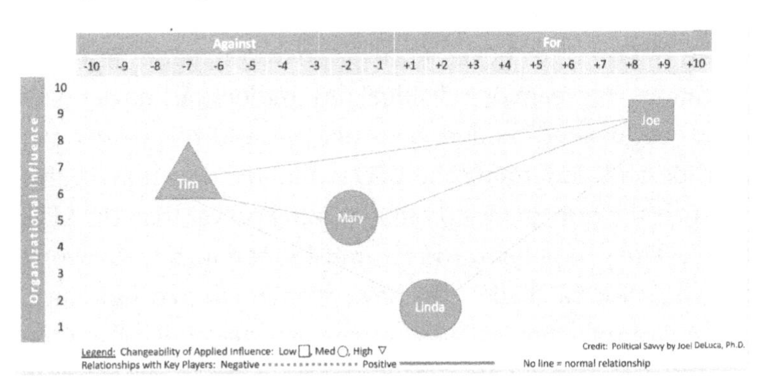

There are several models for creating a Political Landscape map; the book *Political Savvy*[40] details OPMT: The Organizational Politics Mapping Technique. We'll give a quick overview here, but please refer to *Political Savvy* for details and an excellent case study that will provide you with tangible practice.

40 Political Savvy, Joel DeLuca, Ph.D.

4 steps to mapping the Political Terrain:

1. Gather data
2. Quantify
3. Map the Territory
4. Develop a Strategy

When Gathering Data (step 1):

1. Who are the key players?
2. What is their power/influence in the organization?
3. To what extent are they applying their influence for or against the issue?
4. How easily can their applied influence be changed?
5. What significant relationships exist among the key players?

Once you've gathered the data, you'll turn it into a map like this. Again, I'm brushing over some of the process details; please refer to *Political Savvy* for more. Once you have a map, take a look and see where you have opportunities. Maybe someone is connected through some degree of separation that you didn't realize.

And finally, once you have a good picture of your landscape, strategize. Who do you need to focus your influence on? Who can you leverage? Is there a detractor that you can neutralize? Is there a detractor that you were spending too much energy trying to influence? Another insight many people have is that they are not always the right person to do the influencing. In the map above, you might realize that you have no influence over Tim, but Joe does, and Joe trusts you. If we let go of our need to be "the influencer" and our need to be liked, it might be a better strategy to let Joe do the influencing. Tim may never like you, but your transformation work now has support, thanks to Joe.

Journal Exercise: Take a moment to explore your reactions to the words "Politics" and "Power." What's happening in your body when you read these words? What is your relationship with these words? What history and stories do you have around these words? Try letting go of these reactions and let the words just exist, without judging them good or bad. What is possible now?

Strategy and Sequence

When you ask an organization, "Why do you want to Transform?" the answer is rarely the problem you need to solve. I hear things like "we need to stay competitive" or "we need to do more with less." None of these is the real problem, and that's ok. A Transformational Leader meets the organization where it is and guides them to go deeper over time. You'll set a strategy and a sequence for getting them from where they are to where they need to go.

A Transformation Strategy defines the approach and sequence to take the organization from the current reality to the future state. Your strategy depends heavily on the organizational culture, their current pain, and their values. Whether it's top-down, bottom-up, big-bang, or organic, these, and others, are strategic decisions you'll need to make based on an organization's specific context. I've had some clients who value a methodical, scalable approach more than financial results. Their current reality is that they are too far removed from financials to care about them. My strategy was to broadly roll out some simple practices and include a goal-setting practice that connected their work to the financial results. Their economic outcomes didn't matter until they had a methodical approach to see them and impact them. Another client was hyper-focused on preserving cash, so the strategy surgically targeted improvements that would preserve cash quickly. We determined just a few teams to turn super-Agile and focused on prioritizing the overall portfolio of work. Once we slowed the cash leakage, we had the commitment and momentum to expand with organizational-level practices and new teams.

Without the proper sequence, you run the risk of losing support for the transformation. Targeting pain first, finding the adjacent possible, and working through the blockers to the flow of work, are good places to start drafting your sequence. You don't need to plan too far out, just the next few steps, because, with all complex, adaptive systems, your sequence will change and evolve based on what you learn from each step.

Acute Pain. A good place to start a transformational journey is where the organization feels acute pain. We learned earlier that when an organization is experiencing acute pain, they can't hear anything else you say. It's as if they have a nail through their hand, and you want to teach them to meditate. They can't hear you, and you are standing in the way of them getting first aid. Starting with acute pain is a great way to build trust and credibility. Also, don't mistake fire drills for acute pain. If each time you heal acute pain, another acute pain pops up, you might be chasing fire drills, not real fires. Healing true pain makes space for the organization to start moving in the right direction.

Direction is important. When you solve acute pain, be very attuned to whether the solution moves the organization in the right direction. Quick, temporary fixes are fine for acute pain, but when they don't align with the direction, they cause more harm than good. Using the analogy of a nail in the hand, we used to put mercury on those wounds. It was a great antiseptic. We don't do that anymore. 'Nuff said.

The adjacent possible. You might know perfectly well what the real problem is in the organization. If the organization isn't ready to hear it, you're just making noise.

"Tommy, can you hear me?"
- The Who, Tommy

For example, if you're familiar with Agile or lean flow, you might be aware that having too much work in progress slows down the output of an organization. When you walk into an organization with too much work in progress (WIP), you probably feel really smart, and you can just tell them not to work on so many things at once. Go you! When I hear myself using the word 'just,' it's a red flag that I haven't considered my suggestion's impacts. Here's what I've seen, a consultant walks into an organization, and in the first 3 hours, they say, "You need to lower your WIP." In less than 3 hours, the client bounces them out on their butts.

Why?

The organization was not ready to hear it yet. The organization valued multitasking; it measured people on how many balls they kept in the air. A very proud project manager told me that "most project managers can manage five projects, but I can handle eight." Senior management was under pressure to get everything done and more. Everything was important, and everything was urgent; nothing could wait. Telling them not to work on so many things at that point in time was not only noise but also raised their stress level. From their perspective, the consultant was wasting their time with things they couldn't implement. Earlier, we discussed healing the pain; this is the opposite; this consultant was causing pain.
In this example, what might be helpful is adding transparency to the work items so they can start to have productive

conversations around what can and can't get done. Maybe helping them prioritize so that the most important things get done first would reduce some of the pressure people were feeling. Organizations can't limit their work in progress if they can't prioritize. Get them to prioritize first. Often, they don't even know their capacity; "how many work items do we complete in a month?" Helping them know their capacity will help them balance capacity to demand. And then maybe we can start talking about limiting work in progress.

The Sequence of Improving the Flow of Work. I got this wisdom from Dennis Stevens back in 2014, and I've kept it in the notes on my phone, referring to them often. In terms of the practical application of managing the flow of work, here's a cheat sheet on the sequence.

First: Get your system in control:
Balance capacity and demand
Limit WIP (work in progress)
Shrink batch size
Eliminate queues

Second: Optimize your system:
Prioritize the value
Sequence work
Target improvements

The details of these steps are available in Don Reinertsen's seminal work *"The Principles of Product Development Flow."* I'll give you a quick narrative for reference on getting your system in control. Keep in mind, each of these mechanisms comes with a human system.

> *Get your system in control.* "Control" means that there's some equilibrium and predictability for

normal function. The word "control" scared me at first because it made me think we were too controlling, but it really just means bringing it back into the boundaries of expected behavior.

Balance Capacity and Demand. If there's more work coming in than going out, you'll never get ahead. You might have a lot piled up, but let's at least stop the pile from increasing. Now we can forecast. In the previous example, we worked to understand capacity first, and then we worked to prioritize demand. You'll notice that "prioritize the value" comes later. Our attempts to prioritize early were to control the demand, not optimize by priority.

Limit WIP (work in progress). Using Little's formula,[41] determine how much work should be in progress at once to meet the desired cycle time. Keep reducing work in progress until you achieve a smooth flow. No one will let you truly do this, so start by lowering it enough to impact the cycle time. Giving choices like "Do you want both of these work items in 2 weeks or do you want one this week and the second one next week? Either way, you get them both in 2 weeks, but you can have one first if you want." Simplifying the choice will start to embed the concept.

Shrink Batch Size. We use the term "batch" because work moves through a process in a batch. For example, we might collect, or batch, all our code to test on Fridays. Shrinking batch size would mean that maybe I send my code to test every day instead

41 Little Law: Cycle time = WIP / Output rate

of batching it up. Or maybe twice per day.

Big units of work take longer than small units of work. So, make your work unit smaller. Big units require more overhead than small units. And small units that have value can start making or saving money sooner. You'll need some structures to create continuity between small units but look for ways to keep it small. Don Reinertsen gives the example of buying eggs. Buying four dozen eggs at a time creates overhead, takes up space, needs to track expiration dates, etc. But buying one egg at a time might be too small of a batch because I'll need to go to the store seven times per day. Find the right size.

Eliminate Queues. Looking for places where work is piling up is a great place to find inefficiencies. Most of our work nowadays is invisible; it lives somewhere in cyberspace. It's much easier to see queues when it's a box outside your office. By making work visible, using something like a Kanban board, you can clearly see where work is piling up. First, create a cadence by slowing upstream work to meet the capacity of the bottleneck. As illustrated in *The Goal*[42]*, you may create new bottlenecks* when you add resources at the bottleneck. Once you can see the bottleneck, then slowly add resources to places that will improve the flow.

The Roadmap. As a Transformational Leader, someone will ask you to create a "roadmap." People want to see something linear, something with some certainty. I had such an allergic reaction to creating a linear, committed roadmap; I just spun in fury like

42 Eliyahu Goldratt, The Goal

the Tasmanian Devil. "It's not linear! It's not certain!" A client said to me, "I know, you're right, it's not linear, and it's all unknown. But the executives today think linearly. They need to understand where we're going. I know you have some idea of where we're going, and I know you can flatten it to look linear. The roadmap will change as we learn, and that's ok. But you need to do this to move forward." You may not see the future so linearly, but it's the current reality. Meet the organization where it is today. Create a roadmap.

Sample Roadmaps:

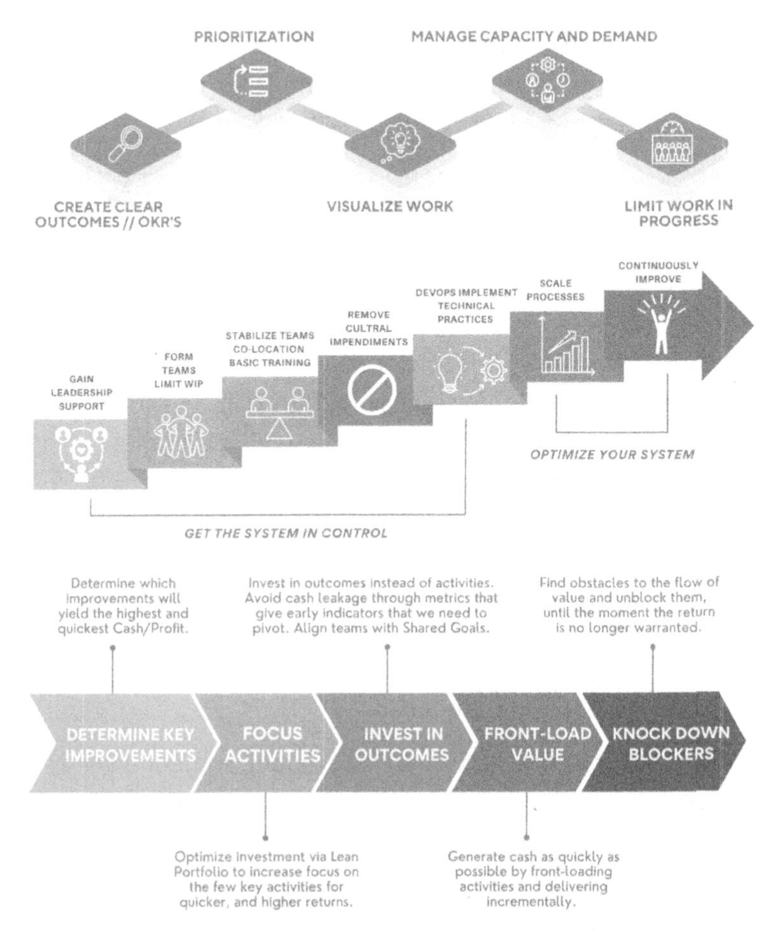

Articulating a clear strategy and sequence will build momentum and enthusiasm for transformation. Strategic clarity will be an anchor for resolving conflict as the organization moves along its journey.

Journal Exercise: Where are you facing resistance in your organization? Get curious about the underlying pain that might be causing this resistance. Can you shift the sequence of your efforts to alleviate some pain?

Organizational Conflict

A lot of literature exists about resolving conflict between individuals. As a Transformational Leader, you'll need to take it up a level; you'll need to resolve conflicts between organizations. Your role is more akin to that of a labor negotiator than a marriage counselor. You might find conflict between departments or with vendors. These conflicts may have been present for years and have become an accepted reality. I often get the dismissive hand wave, "they are non-responsive; they'll never change." As a Transformational Leader, a magic-maker, you are going to do the impossible. You've got to resolve conflicts between departments. Departmental conflict is one of the biggest blockers to Transformation.

Let's take a typical example, Technology Departments (IT) and Product Marketing. Product Marketing has a list of new products and enhancements that they want to launch, but they all require some IT backend updates. I've seen all kinds of conflicts crop up between these two groups in particular. Often there's a conflict in priority because IT serves multiple business teams and lacks a clear way to prioritize between them. The Product Marketing team gets frustrated because they cannot meet their commitments to the company without IT support.

Both the internal and external customers get fewer new features and fewer new products. The organization is less responsive to customer needs. IT gets frustrated with the Product Marketing team because they keep asking for more and more while IT is still working on the last thing. IT rushes the work to quiet the noise, quality goes down, causing even more noise. Walls go up, processes get built, and IT says, 'if you stop talking to us, we'll have more time to get it done. All your communication must go through this one channel, a single point of contact.' Communication shuts down, causing even more disconnection.

How would you solve this conflict between IT and Product Marketing? They appear to be in a vicious cycle. "Just get IT to hire more people." "Just get Product Marketing to stop asking for things." "Just reduce the work in progress." There's that word "just." It's a red flag that shows how these easy answers don't consider the whole system. I'll often draw myself a picture of the conflict as a system. Note: System Diagram notation, also called a 'stock flow diagram,'[43] is excellent for representing these flows, but we'll simplify here for clarity.

43 Donella Meadows, Thinking in Systems, A Primer, 2008.

When you visualize all the impacts on this conflict, you'll see that there are reinforcing feedback loops, feedback that perpetuates the dysfunction. One reinforcing loop is that increased demand for IT results in lower quality, which leads to more demand. You'll also notice another, less direct reinforcing loop around communication. The more communication there is between groups, the longer it takes work to get completed, leading to less communication, which leads to wrong or poor-quality output, which leads to higher demand, perpetuating the cycle.

When you look upstream in the system, you might notice that IT has multiple sources of demand, with no way to prioritize between them. You might hear this expressed as "We have multiple masters; they are all equally important." True, to IT, they are all important, but are they all equally important to the company as a whole? Not as a department, but as a company, what's the priority of each work item? I'm often horrified to find out that by default, IT has the power to prioritize because business units haven't prioritized amongst themselves. IT prioritizing for the whole company is an example of invisible, hidden power sources wielding heavy influence. If the organization doesn't have clear priority and focus, people are left to engage in hand-to-hand combat on the ground.

"When everyone's special, no one is"
- The Incredibles

As a Transformational Leader, how do you approach this conflict? Here's where we dance between soulful and practical. **Feel it, See it, Fix it.**

Feel it. Conflict raises the emotional level. Even though the conflict is systemic, not individual, individuals take on the emotional burden. You've got to address the emotion; otherwise, you end up building processes on top of a garbage heap. When conflict is high, you're walking into a pressure cooker. No one can solve the conflict while tensions are high, so you need to release some pressure before you can do anything. There's nothing to do here besides hold the pain that's in the system. You're creating a space for the group to sit with each other's pain. It is powerful when they start to re-see each other as human beings.

I did this with a group in a room where I couldn't get the chairs in a circle, but they all turned their chairs around to see each other. The first exercise was to go around the room, each person sharing something about the conflict, starting with the phrase[44] "The story I make up about the other department is..." and ending with its impact on them. The beauty of starting with this phrase is that it helps to circumvent blame by acknowledging that we all have some assumptions that might not be accurate. They went around the room, each sharing the pain they felt. One person's voice cracked as they shared their fear of losing their job and relevance because the other group didn't value them. You could have heard a pin drop in this room after they spoke. It's hard not to feel empathy when someone shares their pain with so much vulnerability and courage.

With a small group (10-15), you might simply go around the room and allow each person to speak about how they feel about this conflict and how they feel about the other group, with no interruptions or responses. (Good facilitation techniques will point you to tools for larger groups.) The only access to the organization's emotion is through the individuals, so pull out and name some themes as you hear them. Let the group know

44 Brené Brown, Dare to Lead, 2018.

that there is no need to respond or fix anything yet. Just sit with each other's pain.

See it. In Systems Thinking language, this is known as "revealing the system to itself.[45]" Living systems adapt from within themselves, rather than having change imposed on them. Helping the system see itself is like dusting for fingerprints when suddenly the invisible becomes visible. The word *transparency* describes making the dynamics at play visible. Dennis Pascal, the author of many books on Lean Enterprises, says, "Once you make them visible using basic tools, people say I can't believe we're doing this to ourselves."[46] Systems Thinking diagrams, Polarity Mapping[47] , and simple swim lanes are great tools for visualizing a system. Instead of drawing up a diagram yourself and presenting it to the group, develop the diagram collaboratively. Help them uncover the dynamics that are at play and map them out. Watch them discover and explore the system themselves.

When I'm in person with a group, I like to hang a large sheet of butcher paper on the wall and give the team a lot of space to write. Virtually, online tools like Mural work well for this. With one particularly rigid team, I divided the paper by department and asked them to define what they needed from the other and what they could provide the other. Then they circled the things they needed but weren't getting. Now that it was all visible on the wall, the groups were able to identify the constraints preventing them from giving each other what they needed and get into the next step, fixing it.

45 ORSC – Organizational and Relationship System Coaching, crrglobal.com.
46 Dennis Pascal interview, https://www.lean.org/common/display/?o=1756
47 Polaritypartnerships.com

Fix it. Once the groups see the system and its impact on it, it illuminates new paths to solving it. Solutions will emerge. As a Transformational Leader, you might suggest some tools to consider, but let the team develop their own solution.

"If I had an hour to solve a problem, I'd spend 55 minutes thinking about the problem, and 5 minutes on the solution."
- Albert Einstein

Some great tools that help with hygiene for organizational systems conflict are shared outcomes (OKRs – Objectives and Key Results) and visible prioritization (Lean Portfolio Management). In the example above between IT and Product Marketing, creating an ongoing forum for the business units to create shared outcomes, and prioritize, will drive a cohesive strategy across the business, alleviate conflicting priorities, and free IT from being the 'bad guy."

If you skip the steps of feeling it and seeing it and try to jump into fixing it, you'll find that the fixes won't work. For example, if you jump into OKRs, developing shared outcomes will be impossible because conflict will weave its way into every step. Don't layer a fix on top of a garbage heap.
Using the lens of Organizational Conflict as a System, you'll start to see how the underlying structures can cause or ease conflict. You'll need a new capability to resolve it, and that's where Organizational Coaching and Facilitation play a key role.

Journal Exercise: Where is there conflict between groups in your organization? Do the groups have conflicting goals or beliefs? Draw a diagram of what each group needs from the other and how work flows between them. Can you gain insights on the point of contention? Facilitate a session between the two groups, first asking what assumptions they have about each other and then asking what they need from each other.

Organizational Coaching and Facilitation

A lot of writing exists on the topics of both Coaching and Facilitation. Individual coaching and Group Facilitation are essential tools for every leader to have in their toolbox, so if you aren't familiar with these disciplines, I encourage you to dip your toe in the water.

This section specifically addresses Coaching and Facilitation as it applies at the Organizational level.

Organizational Coaching
In the context of Leading Transformations, let's zoom out from the individual and look at coaching the organization as a whole. The discipline of *Systems Coaching* considers the relationship between the systems, not only the individuals. Organizational Coaching is a type of Systems Coaching, which specifically addresses the need to shift the relationships within an organization and between organizations. As a Transformational Leader, when you see individual behaviors, you are looking beyond the individual. The example of IT and Product Marketing in the previous section on conflict illustrates Organizational Coaching.

Organizational Coaching starts with "revealing the system to itself," which helps the organization become more self-aware. Making the dynamics at play very visible will spark conversation and solutions. A simple example is the Kanban board. A Kanban board is a work management structure with columns showing the state of each work item. A simple Kanban board has columns "to -do, doing and done." When organizations put their work on a Kanban board, the capacity and demand become very visible. Conversations based on personal pressure, stamina, and motivation in the past sounded like, "What can you get done? Make it happen!" now become conversations about system capacity. "We produce four widgets per month, and you're asking us to produce eight this month. We can delay all of them, or you can choose which four you'd like first. We're working to improve so we can do five, but we can't do eight. If we can make five, we'll do the next one."

By making the system visible, we connect the soulful and practical by using the mechanism to remove the burden from the individual. When we ask people to 'take on more' or 'do more with less' it falls squarely on their shoulders with the implication being, 'are you capable?', 'can you handle it?' It's a no-win situation; you have to say yes and work yourself to the bone; otherwise, you are a low performer. Overwhelming the individual depletes energy when we want our organizations to create energy.

Organizational Coaching first reveals the system to itself, then helps the organization adapt. In the example above, the culture drove people to get more work done through incentives, stretch goals, and pressure; "keep calling and asking when will it be done!" Now that we see the system, we can redesign the system from using pressure as a lever to one that uses prioritization and compels us to make hard decisions. As a Transformational Leader, you'll need to help the organization define values and build structures for making trade-off decisions.

Executive Transformation Coaching

We're asking leaders to lead differently, and it all sounds good until the rubber meets the road. Working through specific situations individually with an executive is a game-changer for a Transformation.

Executive Coaching is 1:1 coaching and mentoring that gives leaders space to work through their impact on the Transformation and the Transformation's impact on them. Coaching, in short, means that you help someone work through their challenge by opening up their awareness, not through advice-giving. The core assumption is that they have the answer within them. In a transformation, you might give advice because a coaching session is a safe space to play with new concepts. It's ok to give advice or share knowledge when you need to; just be clear with the person you're coaching that you're switching out of coaching mode.

You may decide to do the coaching yourself or have an outsider perform this role, but you must have coaching; otherwise, executives don't have a lens to see their impact on the organization. To accurately reflect back to leaders what their impact is, it is beneficial to observe them in their "natural habitat," which generally means meetings. Observe their dynamics with their staff, peers, and superiors. One thing I know for sure is that when you talk to someone one-on-one, it's a very different story than what you see in their wild, natural habitat. Some people have a sixth sense for people's impact without even seeing them in the wild. But most of us don't have this sixth sense, and even those that do can be wrong, so get out there and observe what's really happening.

Organizational Facilitation

If our role as Transformational Leaders is to nurture and develop the human system, one of the key conditions we seek is enabling connections between people, better known as collaboration. Collaboration has become a buzzword, so let's be clear on what it means.

Collaboration: Thinking together, such that ideas emerge that don't exist in any single person. In contrast, coordination is arranging pre-existing ideas in sequence; the combined thinking doesn't create anything new.

Collaboration has become popular because it is proven to boost productivity, increase employee engagement, and improve innovation when people work collaboratively.

Mechanistic organizations have suppressed our natural inclination to collaborate. I had someone once tell me, "I hate Agile because it's way too much manual communication." I was confused. I asked, "What is manual communication?" His answer was, "We have to talk to each other!! Why can't all this talking be automated?" There you have it, folks; in a nutshell, this is why we forgot how to collaborate.

Our job as Transformational Leaders is to help people remember how to collaborate and connect with each other. For this, we need facilitation. Marsha Acker gives a great definition of Facilitation.

> *"Facilitation is the ability to guide a group to collaborate from discovery to decision making without dictating the outcome."*
>
> *- Marsha Acker*

Often, we think of facilitation as running a large, collaborative work session. But facilitation tools can help in different forums. Anywhere you have people trying to collaborate, you need facilitation. Your role is to create a safe forum for productive discussion and collaboration.

A professional facilitator will be careful to stay neutral, not to have an opinion; their job is to serve the group's needs. In your role as a Transformational Leader, you're not playing the role of 'professional facilitator'; your facilitation technique needs to be more fluid. Occasionally you might play 'workshop facilitator,' but more often, you'll shift into facilitation mode when the need arises. You won't always be neutral, and you won't always be unattached to the outcome because you are in the game. What you do want is to create a space where all voices are heard and valued, not just your own. Suppose you're in a meeting with peers, and you notice that collaboration seems blocked; people are talking past each other. You'll be bouncing between facilitator and participant. You probably have an opinion, and you are also facilitating. The facilitation people might shun me for saying that, but we've got to account for reality. We can't save our facilitation skills for the perfect forum; we need to weave them into everyday life.

Facilitation attends to a few things in a collaborative discussion:

- Make sure all voices are heard.
- Amplify new ideas, tamp down swirl.
- Serve as the group's memory (i.e., make sure to write things down).
- Reveal the system to itself. Make the invisible become visible.
- Collect and consolidate information/ideas.

There is a whole body of knowledge on facilitation. For more specific tools and information on group facilitation, techniques, please see the resources section.

Journal Exercise: Where is your organizational system lacking the capability to see itself as a system and learn from itself? Where is the organization lacking the capability to collaborate? How might you help the organization see itself as a system?

Organizational Learning

One of the keys to an adaptive organization lies in its ability to learn. Organizations receive information from the external world, make sense of the information, and then synthesize the information internally and learn. The learning is then adopted, applied, and sent to the external world for feedback through the organization's offerings.

A Learning Organization is one where the knowledge lives in the organization, and the organization continually adapts based on learning.

Ever since Peter Senge coined the term "The Learning Organization" back in 1990, people have been talking about becoming one. From what I've observed, we haven't seen many successful moves towards a learning organization. Companies invested huge amounts of money in knowledge management systems after Senge's book came out. It's a Technical Solution to an Adaptive Challenge. They tried to capture all their knowledge in a system.

The result? No one used it.

Why have so many organizations failed to become learning organizations? Two reasons: 1) there is a fundamental misunderstanding on what it means to learn, and 2) we have a lack of patience for learning that doesn't yield immediate value.

Let's explore these blockers and then jump into what it would take to become a true learning organization.

What does it mean to learn? It's a common misunderstanding that learning is equal to training. An HR person once told me, "We're a learning organization; we have a minimum of 40 hours of training per employee per year." Training is not equal to learning. Training is a way of teaching a skill to an individual. Training is what we do to a dog when we teach them to sit. (no offense to our canine pals). Training teaches us how to use a machine or software or use practices to be a better communicator. Learning teaches individuals new ways to think, expands our worldview, exposes us to new perspectives.

Individual learning does not aggregate into organizational learning. The knowledge lives in the organization, not in the heads of the individuals who work there. If we had 100% turnover of staff over time, the organization would still retain the knowledge. Isn't an organization just a collection of individuals? Organizations store knowledge in culture, policy, structure, and capability. As Harley Davidson found out in *The Lean Machine*[48], an individual could know what gauge belts work with which engines, but the organization didn't have a complete picture of that knowledge. If that knowledge is something we 'always ask Joe' or 'figure it out as a one-off each time,' it's not organizational knowledge. In a learning organization, each time we learn, it's fed back into the collective as something everyone knows or is knowable. Only when the knowledge permeates the organization can it then be synthesized and applied.

Once the knowledge is in the organization, the next step is developing the capability to adapt and apply the learning

48 Dantar P. Oosterwal. The Lean Machine: How Harley-Davidson Drove Top-Line Growth and Profitability with Revolutionary Lean Product Development.

quickly. In the early 1990s, many hackers were high-school and college kids who were more interested in demonstrating their power to large institutions than they were in making money or causing harm. Legend has it that a bunch of young hackers broke into the FBI database and stole secret government documents, including the FBI watch list. When the FBI busted them, the FBI watch list was sitting on the hacker's hard drive; the hackers hadn't accessed the file, they never read the list. If they had, they would have seen their own names on it and known they were about to be raided! This story is a classic case of access to information but not effectively learning and adapting.

Remember when we talked about resonance being the seamless transfer of energy between storage types? Reducing all friction between learning and adaptation is another example of this. How seamless is it to move energy between information and implementation? I have trained many people who say, "this training is great, but my boss will never let me do it this way." If not, then why is the organization providing training? We need to address the blockers to adoption before we expect people to uphold it. Otherwise, we are shifting the burden to the individual without committing to systemic change.

What is the value of learning? Have you ever requested training approval and gotten the response "yes, but you better come back and make it worth it by using what you learned." or "provide a report back so everyone can know what you know?" There's often some sense that if you can't use what you learned the minute your butt hits the chair the next day, it was a total waste. The underlying implication here is that learning is frivolous, not real work, not valuable. Some organizations actually categorize learning as a 'perk.' Although training teaches job skills to individuals, organizational learning incorporates knowledge into the organization's DNA over time. It's not a set of facts; it's a shift to new ways of thinking. Individual learning is in service to building an organizational capability that will live beyond the individual doing the learning. We can train individuals on new skills, but collectively we must learn and develop organizational capabilities.

In his Stanford Commencement address, Steve Jobs talks about how he wandered into a class on typography and found it interesting. He didn't know it at the time, but that learning would feed into the fonts for the Mac and later into Word and finally into this book you're reading right now.

> *"[W]e designed it all into the Mac. It was the first computer with beautiful typography. If I had never dropped in on that single course in college, the Mac would have never had multiple typefaces or proportionally spaced fonts."*
> *- Steve Jobs, Stanford Commencement 2005.*[49]

You don't know where the learning is going until you do. There's some trust that, as Steve Jobs says, "the dots will connect." Also, trust that employees aren't just learning for their own frivolous purposes. Set individual learning with the intention of learning in service to the organization.

Organizational Learning means that you need to help the organization learn how to learn, beyond teaching specific skills. You're sowing the garden, not painting each flower. Sowing the garden requires a tremendous amount of trust and faith.

---

49 Stanford Commencement Address 2005, Steve Jobs. https://news.stanford.edu/2005/06/14/jobs-061505/

Journal Exercise: How does your organization learn today? Where can you reimagine learning?

Reframing your Questions

"Forty-two!" yelled Loonquawl. "Is that all you've got to show for seven and a half million years' work?"
"I checked it very thoroughly," said the computer, "and that quite definitely is the answer. I think the problem, to be quite honest with you, is that you've never actually known what the question is."

- Douglas Adams, The Hitchhiker's Guide to the Galaxy

"Organizations evolve in the direction of the questions they most persistently and passionately ask."[50] Before you start looking for answers, you have to know the question. Life moves in the direction of a few simple questions, "How can I survive?", "How can I reproduce?" and maybe a third, "Why are we here." As humans, one or all of those questions guide many of our actions. And if you're thinking, "I don't have kids, I never wanted kids," I don't want to pry, but I'm willing to bet that you enjoy some of the activities designed for reproduction. <Wink> There's no final answer to these questions; the question is answered progressively over time.

US Automakers lost their competitive advantage by asking the wrong questions. In 1984 Japanese car makers were making better, cheaper cars, threatening to put US carmakers out of business. In response, the US put trade restrictions on Japan, forcing them to move some of their manufacturing to the US[51]. These trade restrictions sparked a joint venture between GM and Toyota called NUMMI, a car factory that would sell cars

50 Adapted from Appreciative Inquiry, David Cooperrider.
51 https://www.marketplace.org/2018/11/29/how-us-outgrew-1980s-anxiety-over-japan/

from both brands[52]. GM hoped to learn the Lean Manufacturing practices that had created high efficiency and quality at Toyota, and Toyota was openly willing to share.

In a story about the NUMMI[53] car factory, when representatives from GM visited the Toyota plant in Japan, Toyota was willing to share its secrets. From one of the GM workers who toured the plant:

> "We didn't understand this bigger picture thing. All of our questions were focused on the floor, you know? The assembly plant. What's happening on the line. That's not the real issue. The issue is, how do you support that system with all the other functions that have to take place in the organization?"[54]

Asking the wrong questions caused a decades-long delay in American car manufacturers from leveraging the success of the Japanese carmakers.

What are the big questions your organization is seeking to answer? When it comes to transformation, these questions take some digging. Don't stop at the first question that pops up; keep peeling it back to look for the question that drives action. What are the real Adaptive Challenges you face? Is the question framed in a way that suggests a technical solution, where an adaptive approach is more appropriate? I told the NUMMI story to the executive who visited Google and came away with the idea that they should only have four programming languages. They couldn't imagine what other questions they could have asked.

Usually, I hear things like this on the surface:

---

52 Wikipedia: https://en.wikipedia.org/wiki/NUMMI

53 This American Life, NUMMI, . https://www.thisamericanlife.org/561/nummi-2015

54 This American Life, NUMMI, . https://www.thisamericanlife.org/561/nummi-2015

At the Organizational Level:

- How can we beat our competition?
- How can we gain more market share?
- How can we increase revenue?
- How can we drive down costs?
- How do we improve innovation?
- How do we improve employee productivity? (currently disguised as 'engagement')

At the Departmental Level:

- How do we get buy-in for the Transformation?
- How do we scale the change to new ways of working?
- How do we get our partner organizations to align with our goals?

What do you notice about these questions? They seem to imply that there's "an answer," one best answer or maybe a few. There's a sense with some of the questions that there's a checkbox or completion date. Perhaps you can get a consultant to help roll out an initiative to address the issue. I have shifted to the word *inquiry* because I've found that the word 'question' causes people to feel compelled to jump to a quick answer. The term 'inquiry' seems to allow a little more room for exploration.

Here are some questions that might spark more action, more learning. Don't use these; come up with your own. These are just examples.

At the Organizational Level:

- How can we better help our customers feel better

about themselves? (This is product-line dependent; this might work for a makeup / clothing / fitness company).
- How can we ensure that we are adapting to our environment?

Notice with these questions; they never reach completion. You can continue to ask this question and use it as a guide forever. The company might always be looking for ways to help customers feel better. You'll always look for ways to be adaptive. With something like "beating the competition," once you are #1, what do you do? You need to change the question.

At the departmental level, and for the purpose of this book, let's specifically look at the Transformation Team level:

- How can we best serve the future of this company?
- What capabilities do we need to build to help the company be self-adaptive?

I once pissed off a lot of people by stating "The question is not 'how do we make the organization Agile?' The question is 'how do we make them successful?'" The pushback I got was that "there are a lot of ways to help them be successful, but we're Agilists. If something better comes along, it sounds like you're ready to kick Agile to the curb!" Exactly. In the accusation was the answer, the source of what I was trying to avoid. *"If something better comes along."* The implication was that they weren't going to be distracted by something better. I wanted them to be distracted by something better! If something better came along, shouldn't we consider it? The problem was a clash between the Technical Solution and the Adaptive Challenge. If we stay focused on our current solution, we miss the opportunity to apply a better solution based on what we've learned. Broad inquiry questions keep the organization open to more possibilities.

Journal Exercise: What are the big questions your organization is asking? Are those questions serving the organization or limiting it? What questions might expand the organization into new possibilities?

Budget, Capacity and Resource Allocation

Budget, capacity, and resource allocation are all ways that we inject energy into our organization. It's fuel for creating value; without money, people, and time you have no fuel, nothing gets done. When we get lost in the minutiae of a process, we can lose the connection to the process's true purpose, creating energy to feed the organization's soul. When we get lost in budget meetings, it's easy for the process to become a proxy for the company's soul, and it can appear as a very bleak soul.

"How do we know our capacity?" "How do we manage resource allocation?" "What about budgeting?" How do we know our capacity when we're in this world of a living, self-organizing system? How do we know if we need to add or reduce our staff? I'm going to get tactical in a moment and address the current reality. But before I do that, let's apply the 5 Steps to Soul to connect back into why we do budget planning in the first place.

The 5 Steps to Soul applied to Budget Planning

> ***1. What is the soulful purpose?***
> We do budget planning to optimize the organization's investment to get the best outcome from the lowest expenditure of energy. We might also include maintaining our own livelihood.

2. What makes it soul-crushing?

Budget planning can take up an enormous amount of time and energy that takes people away from getting the work done. There is also uncertainty about whether the budget will be approved, putting people's teams and work at risk.

3. Where does it violate Power, Freedom, and Connection?

Budget planning violates people's power when they submit their budget proposal then sit in the dark and wait for approval from their superiors. There is often little freedom to alter the budget process, move money between peers or creatively fund your own initiative. Once funded, there is little freedom to spend the money without further approval and constraints. Budget planning can violate peer connection when it pits people against each other in a zero-sum game.

4. What tensions are at play?

The budget process typically brings several tensions to the surface as the organization decides where to invest. Some common tensions are long-term & short-term, stability & change and exploitation & innovation.

5. What would it take to bring in soul?

When organizations reimagine budget planning, they might move from funding activities to funding outcomes, shorten the budget cycle, and separate funding from people's personal agendas. In the next section, we'll explore an option to decouple prioritization, capacity, and funding.

The problem is that there is tremendous entropy (energy leaked) in budget planning itself. The goal is to shift the energy expended in managing budget, capacity, and resource allocation and move that energy towards the outcomes. Why is so much energy leaking? There's a secondary goal in funding, capacity, and resource allocation, and that goal is control. The cost of control is not justifying the return. Let's explore where we can get energy back from the process and minimize the downside risk of losing some control.

Decoupling Prioritization, Capacity, and Funding.[55]

It's in vogue today to move to more frequent, outcome-based budgeting. *Frequent* means quarterly or on-demand funding. *Outcome-based* means that we invest in outcomes instead of deliverables. These solutions are useful, but they won't work unless the organization addresses the underlying problem of muddling **Prioritization, Capacity, and Funding.**

> "We budgeted for it, so it's prioritized!"
> "We were clear about the five priorities for this year, so why are people still having priority questions?"
> "We budgeted and prioritized, but I can't get people to work on it!"

To get value from any modern budgeting practices, you first need to decouple (or 'de-triple') these three activities. If you increase budgeting frequency without decoupling, you've just increased the frequency of your confusion.

You've become outcome-driven, but no one can meet the outcomes. You've increased workplace frustration ten-fold because now we are scrambling to find capacity all the time.

55 https://www.rosettatg.com/blogtoon/2019/9/29/decoupling-budget-capacity-and-prioritization

This model simplifies the *budget grind*[56] many companies face. The *budget grind* is when companies spend the whole year fussing over budget numbers because the priority and capacity are implicit in the budget. When you decouple these activities, the entire budget process becomes more straightforward.

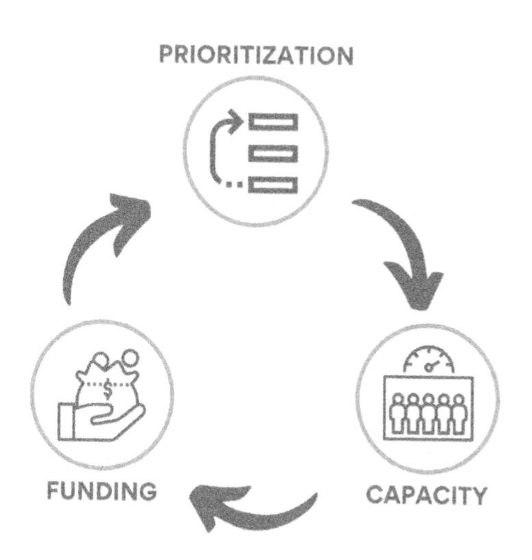

1. **Prioritization.** Stop talking about funding and capacity until you prioritize the outcomes you want across the organization. When you have your priorities, you need to put them in order. Yes, even high-level strategic goals need to be in priority order. Why? Because people will have to make trade-offs, and they need the principles to make the decision.

   For example:

   "We are supposed to be customer-focused, but we are also supposed to cut costs, so should I give this customer a refund or not?"

56 For those of you aware of my objection to the word 'grind'; Hypocrisy acknowledged. I couldn't think of a better word. Suggestions welcome.

"I'm working on something strategic, but I was called into an operational issue today that will delay the strategic work. Which should I focus on?"

2. **Capacity**. With old-school capacity planning, we would act as chess masters of resource allocation, estimate all work and plan people's time down to the hour. Resource planning is about who is going to work on that first item on your priority list. And then the second one. And maybe the third. Until your capacity is full for the time being. Don't plan out the year, plan the moment.

   Does capacity mean individuals or teams? Yes. Start by planning capacity by teams; it's way easier than planning for individuals. You may find that your current team structure no longer serves the needs of your portfolio, so you'll have to tweak it, maybe add/remove teams.

3. **Funding**. Once you have prioritized and planned capacity and you're ready to go, then allocate funding. Funding is the very last thing we do, allowing money to be free and flexible as long as possible.

What frequency should we budget? Ideally, you want to budget as infrequently as possible but frequently enough to respond to business needs. Don't try and do more frequent budgeting if you don't need to; it's a waste of energy. Some companies have a mechanism to create on-demand budgeting if there's a need between cycles. I assert that even if you stay with your current budget process, decoupling budget from prioritization and capacity gives you a staggering improvement in outcomes.

Capacity and Resource Allocation

We need to know our capacity and resources so that we can forecast and plan. Some popular management trends out there say we don't need a forecast or a plan, and perhaps there's some future state where we all live in the moment. But for now, the current reality is that we need to know if we need to staff up or ramp down because hiring and attrition are long cycles.

To know our capacity and supply the correct number of people to do the work, we must radically change our view of capacity and resource allocation. Note: I am aware that we shouldn't call people 'resources'; I'm starting with the current reality, then we'll move into the future state.

Capacity is the amount of work or value a team can complete as a function of time. With the same number of people, capacity can change over time. Improvements to capability and technology can impact capacity. Capacity is great for forecasting and planning.

Is this definition different than your current definition? Traditionally, we have looked at capacity as the "number of person-hours." The problem with that definition is that it requires people to translate work into effort estimates, and work estimates have a huge margin of error. When we estimate hours, we miss all kinds of variables like task switching cost, administrative time, and buffer time. We spend energy trying to get more precision in the output than the accuracy of the input. (remember significant digits in high school math? The result can't have more precision than the input variables.)

By looking instead at our actuals, we can map work to our capacity as a unit.

"If we produce ten widgets per month, you can forecast for ten widgets per month. We'll work on improving it to eleven, but until we see the results of our improvements, please forecast for ten. If we have time after the 10th, we'll do an 11th."

The energy we spent on estimating and arguing about what could or could not get done all goes away. Pressure about "figure out a way" and "make it happen" goes away. Insistence on doubling workload becomes a transparent conversation about time. Doubling workload will at a minimum double the time, likely more like 2.5x, and the time increases exponentially as the workload moves further beyond capacity.[57]

Resource allocation becomes very simple when we view capacity in this way. In the above example, if we need to increase our widget production to 20, we'd need to double our staff. Of course, it's not linear that way, but you have some idea for forecasting.

I worked with an organization that added 600 people to increase capacity, resulting in an actual decline in output. Of course, the 600 people increased overhead and ramp-up capacity, but that wasn't the problem. The problem was that they added people based on manager requests, where managers could argue that they were short-staffed. Unfortunately, those were not the constraint points[58]. For example, suppose I add people to a programming team because they have a growing work queue. I might find out that alleviating that queue will move the queue to the next downstream team, perhaps the test team. Until I

57 For more on optimizing work flow see Don Reinertsen's Principles of Product Development Flow

58 For more on the Theory of Constraints see Eliyahu Goldratt's The Goal

know the capacity of the organization and the capacity of each team, I am shooting in the dark when I hire people. We need to know the capacity through the ecosystem and carefully add at the constraint points where capacity will enable flow.

Another failure mode for resource allocation is increasing capacity for work that doesn't impact the output or the outcome. In the previous example, people may have been very busy, but if their work was feeding an internal process that didn't enable flow, it had no impact on the outcome. To be clear, this is perfectly fine if your objective is something other than increasing output, such as risk reduction or employee happiness. But if your goal directly impacts ROI, you want to match expanded capacity with activities that affect output.

The final myth about resource allocation is that it can be managed and controlled in a granular way. Those tools that allow you to be like a chess master, controlling every move, controlling people's time down to the hour, these tools seem to have forgotten the cost of task-switching. Allocating someone to one project for 8 hours is not the same as allocating someone to 8 projects for one hour each. The chart below shows the productivity loss due to context switching. When working on five simultaneous projects, you lose 75% of your time to context switching. 75% entropy, 25% actual work gets done. Now consider what happens when a team is context switching. For one, it's hard to get everyone into a meeting at the same time! And when we do have a meeting, someone is distracted or can't make it. More entropy results because we have task-switching at the organizational level.

NUMBER OF SIMULTANEOUS PROJECTS	PERCENT OF TIME AVAILABLE PER PROJECT	LOSS TO CONTEXT SWITCHING
1	100%	0%
2	40%	20%
3	20%	40%
4	10%	60%
5	5%	75%

Credit: Quality Software Management by Gerald Weinberg and Roger Brown, Infoq.

The bottom line on resource allocation is this: get a clear picture of capacity before you add a single person to your organization. Ramp up and ramp down based on actual capacity and capability needs that drive the organization's strategy and goals. Generally, don't add people based on a request from an overworked team until you've found out why they are overworked. And finally, don't try and be a chess-master when it comes to resource allocation; add people where they are needed and let them self-organize to get the work done.

Journal Exercise: Is your organization's budget planning process effective? Where does tackling budget planning fit in the strategy and sequence for your transformation? How might you take simple steps to decouple budget discussions around prioritization, capacity, and funding?

Measuring Transformations

"Statistics [Metrics] are used much like a drunk uses a lamppost: for support, not illumination."

- Vin Scully

The only valid reason to measure anything is to decide on action or inaction based on the result. Using Step 1 of **The 5 Steps to Soul in the Workplace,** the soulful purpose of metrics is to learn and make positive adjustments. Metrics get soul-crushing when we use them to prove our self-worth.

In the current reality, your organization may want to know how they can tell if you're doing a good job. Here's a secret for you, companies don't know how to judge a transformation. If left to their own devices, they'll judge it using old measurements. But if you show them how to evaluate, they'll likely accept your measuring criteria. The key is to have the answer ready. Teach them to judge you on the right metrics. You need to shift the metrics from judging who is 'doing a good job' to metrics that drive decisions for the organization. The best way to measure success is through tangible results, and in business, that usually means money.

Show me the Money. If yours is not a business driven by money, substitute whatever it is. Maybe it's the number of elephants saved. But mostly, it's money. If you want to measure your transformation, show me the money. "But my transformation is about more than money!" Money may not be the ultimate goal; however, money talks if you want to stay in the game. Do you want power so you can do the things you need to do? Money is the fuel that keeps an organization running.

Don Reinertsen tells a story about people waiting in line outside his office.

> "As a business owner, I have two lines outside my office. The line on the right has people wanting me to spend money; vendors selling me something, employees wanting me to fund their idea, teams wanting new equipment, etc. This line on the right is really long. The line on the left contains people wanting to help me make money. There's hardly anyone on that line, and the wait is really short. If you want my attention, I suggest you figure out a way to get in the line on the left."

Don Reinertsen's story connects metrics with buy-in and executive communication. Asking for money gives you very little power but showing you can make money or other positive outcomes will put you in a position of strength. Metrics are your friend because demonstrating that positive outcome will create a virtuous cycle of transformation.

Metrics cut through the mess. I told you a story earlier about an Agile Transformation that was messy and seemed to be floundering. Still, the organization met its yearly financials in only six months, effectively doubling the financial goal for the year. As the Transformation Lead, I continually re-directed the team to the results. Without those numbers, I would have been sunk. If the organization had based its assessment on how it felt, it would not have continued. It felt messy and disorganized. But because we had the numbers, specifically in dollars, they stuck with it.

The staggering financials created hope, momentum, inspiration. I was able to use those metrics to leverage even more improvements. I said, "You're right, it is a mess, and we've doubled our financials. Just imagine what those financials will look like when we get better at Agile!" And I would take them to the adjacent possible next step. I kept creating connections between the changes they were making and the results they were seeing. I didn't need to prove causation; correlation, in this case, was enough because they had unprecedented results. It was exhilarating, and people would rather build on it than analyze why it happened.

But you can't wait until the results roll in; you need some metrics to show that you are heading in the right direction. And you need to know that the organization is healthy, so you're not getting results by burning out the organization.

AgilityHealth[59] recommends balancing metrics in these three buckets:

- Health & Maturity (Qualitative - Leading):
  Are we developing the capabilities that we think we need?
- Delivery /Performance (Quantitative - Leading): Are we getting the stuff done that we think is important?
- Business Outcomes (Lagging): Is all the stuff we thought would work, actually working?

Leading indicators show that you are doing what you think is going to work. The lagging indicator shows whether it actually worked. The more you can link these two together, the better.

59 AgilityHealth.com

Credit: https://www.rosettatg.com/blogtoon/2018/7/10/the-problem-with-metrics

Design Metrics that Disprove your Hypothesis. Traditionally, leaders have used metrics to show that they were successful. We even called them "success metrics," also known as "vanity metrics." If you've been around the corporate world for a minute, you know that success metrics always show success. I had an executive say to me, "Based on the status updates, everything seems rosy, but then why are our finance numbers down?"The problem is that they designed metrics were to make themselves look good while keeping the executives happy and feeling in control. While 'vanity metrics' may benefit your career, unfortunately, they are not valuable for the organization.

"The first principle is that you must not fool yourself, and you are the easiest person to fool."

- Richard Feynman

The questions you need metrics to answer are "How will you know when you're wrong?" and "How will you know if you need to change direction or cut losses?" You need to define those metrics and thresholds before you are invested in the outcome. I don't want to know that you're doing what you said you would do; I want to know if what you said you would do has the impact you thought it would. We are terrible at making that judgment call about our babies, so we need to make it clear before we start.

Metrics are not All-Inclusive. Have you ever received a set of metrics that made your eyes hurt? It's a myth that we need metrics to cover every possible outcome and explanation. We end up with reams of data, and everyone has a different interpretation. Instead, design your metrics to tell you where to look, to spark further analysis. Your metrics should be broad enough that an anomaly shows up, but you need to dig into it to find out why. For example, instead of giving me sales by region, district, customer, and product, just start by looking at whether sales are up or down and whether there are any outliers. If sales are flat and there are no outliers, I don't need to know anything else. If sales are down 10%, then we look at what's driving the drop.

Keep your Metrics at the right level of Granularity. Metrics get muddled when they are at the wrong level of granularity for the audience. For example, metrics on team-level tasks are not meaningful to the C-Suite. And conversely, metrics on big corporate investments may be interesting but are not actionable to delivery teams.

Metrics dashboards connect layers of granularity, as well as show the balancing metrics side-by-side. One client used this template to connect features with portfolio-level outcomes.

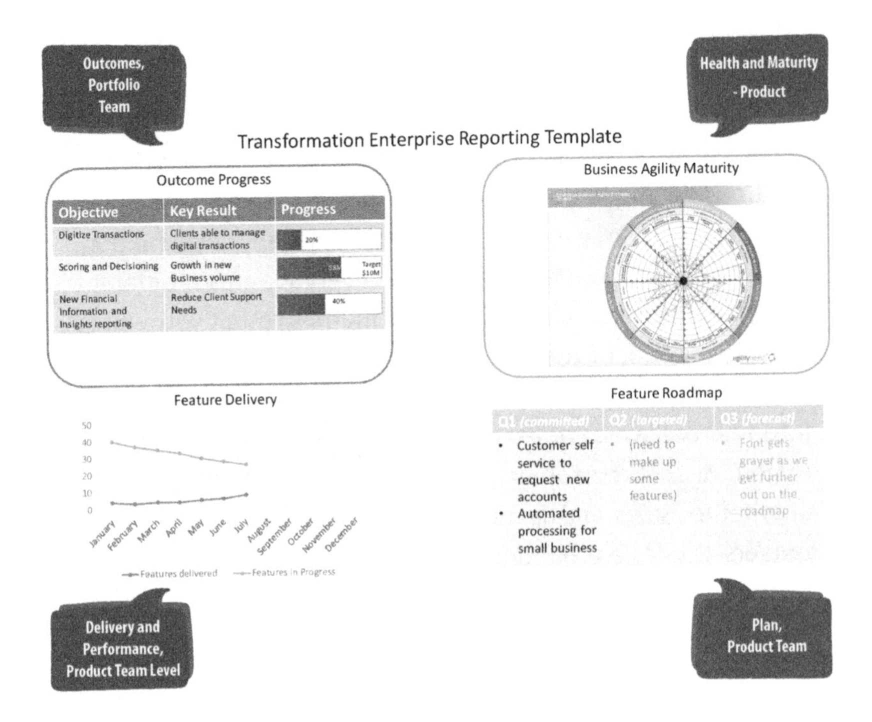

Metrics are handy when we use them to learn, but they are soul-crushing when used to rank and judge people's value.

Journal Exercise: What metrics are dominant in your organization today? What is the purpose of these metrics? (i.e., drive behavior, drive performance, inform decisions). How might you design and incorporate more balanced metrics for decision-making?

Organizing for Adaptability: Key Takeaways

I'll never forget the day when I saw a client show the first sign of Organizational Adaptability. I was sitting in a meeting where Patrice asked her peers for feedback on requesting additional funding from upper management. Patrice was a brilliant woman, but her frenetic energy and wild gesticulations could exhaust a meeting. When she started to speak, I could feel the rest of the room take a mental check out. That is until Ben spoke up. Ben was a young, bookish hipster, new to the team. He was usually calm and quiet, but when he cleared his throat, we knew that he would change the trajectory of the meeting with a few well-placed words. He said, "Patrice, what you're doing is important. I have budget for Q3 and Q4, and I don't know if I'll need it. Why don't you take it now, and if I need it later, then we'll talk about going up the ladder for more funding." It was as if time stood still. Patrice was stunned into a rare moment of speechlessness. No one had ever offered to share their budget with a peer before. Ben finally spoke up and said, "Why are you all looking at me? Isn't this the whole point of Agility?" With a few words, Ben had set a precedent that catapulted the team into adaptability. They would never be the same.

The team had transcended past the need to protect their turf and looked more broadly at the organization. They were well on their way to becoming an adaptable organization.
I was only able to help this organization become adaptable by starting with myself. Once I got my own baggage out of my way and mastered my domain, I could better connect with people. By connecting with other people, we were able to co-create better systems. I would have been of no help to Ben, Patrice, and their team if I was busy trying to be right and force a process on them. I was able to be effective because I had done the hard work on myself first and the work with others second.

Seeing teams like Ben and Patrice's start to flourish makes my heart sing.

Journal Exercise: What have you learned about the system of organizations? Where will you explore further to help your organization adapt?

Key Takeaways:

- **Emergence and Thriving, Living Systems:** Viewing organizations like living systems and less like machines allows them to expand into new possibilities. Living systems have three essential properties: self-organization, resilience, and natural hierarchy.
- **Organizational Tensions:** Well-managed tensions can be generative and create advancement; poorly managed tensions can create dysfunction and oscillation.
- **Adaptive Challenges:** Transformational work is an adaptive challenge, don't treat it like a technical problem.
- **Systems Thinking:** Transformational leaders consider the overall system and its impacts rather than reducing it to its components. The intelligence of a system is in the interconnectedness, not the parts.
- **Correlation is Not Causation:** Be wary of copying the success of other organizations by imitating their output. The output is correlated to their success, but it's not the cause.
- **Organizational Emotional Intelligence:** The same capabilities that build individual emotional intelligence can apply to the organization, including identity, self-awareness, emotional literacy, curiosity, courage, resiliency, and recovery.
- **The Soulful Organization:** A 5-step process can bring soul to soulless situations.

    1. *What is the soulful purpose?*
    2. *What makes it soul-crushing?*
    3. *Where does it violate Power, Freedom, and Connection?*

4. *What tensions are at play?*
5. *What would it take to bring in soul?*

- **Power Dynamics and Politics:** Transformational leaders know how to navigate the human system.
- **Strategy and Sequence:** The strategy and sequence of changes are unique to each organization. Creating clarity around strategy and sequence is key.
- **Organizational Conflict:** Conflict at the organizational level is usually systemic or structural. Feel it, see it, fix it.
- **Organizational Coaching and Facilitation:** Transformational leaders help the system learn from itself by coaching and facilitating the organization as a whole.
- **Organizational Learning:** Organizational learning is the capability to accept new information, make sense of it, synthesize, and apply it. Organizational Learning is different from individual learning and skill training.
- **Reframing your Questions:** Broadening your questions can open up more possibilities for the answer.
- **Budget, Capacity, and Resource Allocation:** Decouple prioritization, capacity, and funding.
- **Measuring Transformations:** Focus on outcomes but balance with performance and health. Design metrics that can disprove hypotheses.

WHERE DO WE GO FROM HERE?

When I started on this journey, my goal was to stay in the box, and it was a nice box. Maybe a box with windows and a mini-fridge. As I moved into bigger and bigger boxes, I realized that it wasn't me that needed to change; it was the boxes that had to go.

I had been trying to accumulate knowledge because if I could just know that one more thing, I would be … I would be what exactly? Successful? Change the world? But all those books I was reading hadn't changed the world yet, so how would my reading them change the world?
A few years ago, I made a resolution not to read for the year on New Year's Day. Yes, while most people resolve to read a lot of books, I resolved to read none. When I called my friend to tell her about my reverse-new year's resolution, she said, "Good. You know enough." She was right; it was time to stop consuming and start sharing, start creating. I only made it until mid-February with my resolution (perhaps I have a problem), but something shifted inside me. I slowed my reading. I stopped reading for the purpose of seeking answers and started reading for contemplation. I no longer rushed through books, desperate for information, which I quickly forgot anyway. I now meandered through books, enjoying the ideas and sometimes re-reading them.

This experience changed me; it changed my worldview. It marked a shift from seeing myself as a "knower" to seeing myself as a "catalyst." Just like Dorothy in the Wizard of Oz, I found out I'd had the power all along. I'd always been a catalyst; I just didn't see it. Once I started to see myself differently, I could lean into being a truly transformational leader.

As I sit here, during a pandemic, a time of so much uncertainty, the one thing I know for sure is that we need Transformational Leaders to lead into and through change. We're seeing the impact of a world that has spent far too long keeping people contained in the box of "compliant employee" and has atrophied our collective ability to adapt. It's time to unleash the power of each whole human being and the power of what we can be when we work together in a natural way.

I pass the challenge on to you. Take a break from trying to find answers and go make a difference. There's no certification, no book, no webinar that is going to give you the answer. You're ready. The time is now.

You know enough.

Further Learning

Marsha Acker. *The Art and Science of Facilitation. 2020.*

Lyssa Adkins. *Coaching Agile Teams. 2010.*

Brené Brown. *Dare to Lead: Brave Work. Tough Conversations. Whole Hearts. 2018.*

W. Edwards Deming. *The New Economics; For Government, Industry and Education. 1994.*

Aaron Dignan. *Brave New Work: Are You Ready to Reinvent Your Organization? 2019.*

Wayne Dyer. *21 Days to Master Success and Inner Peace. 2011.*

Robert Fritz. *The Path of Least Resistance for Managers. 2011.*

Eliyahu Goldratt, *The Goal: A Process of Ongoing Improvement. 1992.*

Phil Knight. *Shoe Dog: A Memoir by the Creator of Nike. 2018.*

Gary Hamel. *The Future of Management. 2007.*

Dantar P. Oosterwal. *The Lean Machine: How Harley-Davidson Drove Top-Line Growth and Profitability with Revolutionary Lean Product Development. 2010.*

Donald G. Reinertsen. *The Principles of Product Development Flow. 2009.*

David Rock. *Your Brain at Work. 2009.*

Anne Rød; Marita Fridjhon, *Creating Intelligent Teams. 2016.*

Margaret Wheatley:
Margaret Wheatley, Who Do We Choose to Be? 2017.

Margaret Wheatley, *The Irresistible Future of Organizing (article). 1996*

More Margaret Wheatly links here:
https://margaretwheatley.com/library/articles/

Videos:
Inner Workings: Pixar, 2016. (shown before Moana)

Inno-versity Presents: Greatness by David Marquet.
https://www.youtube.com/watch?v=psAXMqxwol8

Made in the USA
Middletown, DE
06 October 2022